THE LAST HOUR

Discerning the End Times-A Biblical Perspective

D1712766

BINIAM DEBEBE

This book is dedicated to
Jesus Christ – the King of Kings; the Lord of Lords; the
Alpha and Omega; the Wonderful Counselor; the Mighty
God; the Everlasting Father; the Prince of Peace; the
Bread of Life; and the Way, the Truth, and the Life!

CONTENTS

FOREWORD

Brother Biniam's book *"The Last Hour Discerning the End Times – A Biblical Perspective"* is exactly that. It is a book with many prophetic or end times Scriptures, which he ties to past and current events. As you read this book, you will learn many interesting and relevant facts pertaining to "the Last Days" and "the End Times". In this book he has taken special care to not predict when Christ will return for His church, or to predict whether this event will happen before, during, or after the "Great Tribulation." The purpose of his book is to make you aware through Scriptures, and past and current events, that the "End Times" are at hand and how to be prepared for them. I am sure you will receive a lot from reading his book.

Rev. Larry Brown
Founder and President of Turning Point Ministries (TPM),
P.O. Box 2981, Broken Arrow, OK 74013-2981
www.turningpointmin.org

In this book, the author opens the Scriptures about the second coming of Jesus Christ. He described all the events from the Scriptures in chronological order so that everyone can understand them. Overall, the book is well researched and gives more clarity and deep insight into God's mind and purpose of Jesus' second coming. It is a great book. I highly recommend to everyone.

Dr. Emmanuel Haile,
Pastor at International Ethiopian Evangelical Church,
Washington, DC

PREFACE

The Apostle John wrote, "Dear children, this is the last hour; and as you have heard that the antichrist is coming, even now many antichrists have come. This is how we know it is the last hour" (1 John 2:18). He wrote this message or the Epistles of John to Christian believers, hence the reference "dear children". The Apostle John wrote to those Christians who lived in western Asia Minor so that they might not be ignorant of the things to come in the end times including:

- To promote fellowship of believers (1 John 1:3);
- To share the joy with believers that the Apostle John and the other disciples received in Jesus (1 John 1:4);
- To induce holiness among believers (1 John 2:1);
- To prevent heresy (apostates) (Gnosticism of the first century);
- To discern the end times (1 John 2:18 & 2:26);
- To encourage Christians to continue to believe and to be persistent in the faith so that they may be unashamed, spotless, and without wrinkle (1 John 2:28); and finally
- To inform believers regarding the promise of eternal life (1 John 5:13).

Jesus started His ministry on earth by proclaiming that "the kingdom of God is near" (Mark 1:15). He also said, "When you see a cloud rising in the west, immediately you say, 'It's going to rain,' and it does. And when the south wind blows, you say, 'It's going to be hot,' and it is. Hypocrites! You know how to interpret the appearance of the earth and the sky. How is it that you don't know how to interpret this present time?" (Luke 12:54-56).

In this passage, Jesus emphasizes the importance of interpreting the times through faith by listening to and believing what God has said about the end times rather than just believing what we see happening around us. God wants us to be informed about things before they happen so that we are aware and forewarned. We discern future events only by faith in Jesus Christ and not with our physical eyesight. "Now faith is being sure of what we hope for and certain of what we do not see." (Hebrews 11:1). Faith is much like a magnifying glass that allows us to look at things far into the future. After receiving it from His Father, Jesus revealed the end times plan to us, so we could be prepared for what was to come. This is evident from the book of Revelation. The Apostle John received the revelation of Jesus Christ from the angel and wrote the message of Jesus to the church and believers.

John the Baptist also said, "You brood of vipers! Who warned you to flee from the coming wrath?" (Matthew 3:7). In this passage, John the Baptist addressed the Pharisees and Sadducees who rejected both the message that Jesus was the Messiah and warnings about the coming kingdom of God. Because they refused to hear the truth, the Pharisees and Sadducees missed the visitation of God through His Son, Jesus Christ. John the Baptist also warned the Pharisees and

Sadducees by saying, "The ax is already at the root of the trees" (Matthew 3:10). In other words, the kingdom of God is near.

In addition, the Apostle Paul warned the saints of the church of Ephesus to be very careful because the days were evil, even back in the first century AD. He then reminded them not to be foolish but to be wise and to understand "what the Lord's will is" (Ephesians 5:17). It is tragic when our eyes are blind and our ears are deaf to what God is trying to communicate to us. The Apostle Paul also reminded us to understand the present time (Romans 13:11) and to wake up because our salvation is nearer than when we first believed in Jesus Christ.

Many people are confused about the second coming of Jesus because of various conflicting prophecies and reports they have heard. Some, like the Thessalonians, even thought that the day of the Lord had already come (2 Thessalonians 2:1-2). The Apostle Paul again warned us not to be deceived because the end will not come until the antichrist is revealed (2 Thessalonians 2:3).

Therefore, it is important to interpret the times by the power of the Holy Spirit. The purpose and main theme of this book is to help believers discern the end times or the last hour from a biblical perspective. The importance of discerning the end times include:

- Avoiding the confusion and deception about the second coming of Jesus;
- Discerning and recognizing the antichrists and false prophets of our times;
- Understanding the importance of voicing our concerns over and praying for the persecuted church;

- Understanding the importance of witnessing to others about Jesus *"as long as it is day"* (John 9:4), or while we have the opportunity;
- Being watchful and in prayer, and understanding what the plan and will of God is so we do not miss His promises;
- Being saved from the coming wrath of God and escaping eternal death; and finally
- Holding onto the hope of salvation and standing firm in the faith, during the end times or in times of trouble.

Matthew's Gospel and the prophetic Books of Daniel, Ezekiel, Joel, Zechariah, and Revelation are the key books in the Holy Bible to understanding about the end times. This book will mainly focus on what Jesus said about the signs of the end times and His second coming (the day of the Lord) according to Matthew 24, also called the Olivet Discourse.

PART 1:
THE LAST HOUR

"Dear children, this is the last hour; and as you have heard that the antichrist is coming, even now many antichrists have come. This is how we know it is the last hour."
(1 John 2:18)

CHAPTER 1:
WHAT IS THE LAST HOUR?

The phrase "*last hour*" is a synonym for the "*last time*", and it means the "*end of time*" or "*end times*". The word "*last*" is mentioned fifty five times and the word "*hour*" is mentioned fifty two times in the New Testament of the Holy Bible. In Greek, the word "*last*" is "*eschatos*" or the "*end*" while the word "*hour*" is "*hora*". The word "*hour*" is defined as certain definite time or season fixed by natural law. The two words combined form the phrase "*last hour*" to mean the "*end times*".

Currently, there are many books written by various authors who predict what happens in the end times. These include: date-setters like the 2012 doomsday believers, philosophers, Bible code researchers, non-believers, politicians, and others. Most of these writers were far more interested in shaping the Scriptures to fit their own personal beliefs than in shaping their personal beliefs to fit the Scriptures.

Therefore, we should not be confused or deceived by anyone about the end times. The important thing to remember is who is telling the truth and are we ready for the truth? There is one and only one true source that we can search the truth about the end times from—the Holy Bible! To understand what is created, we need to know first who the creator is.

We must seek the word of God for the truth, unlike many others, because God is the one and only Creator of all things and Jesus is the author of life. "In the beginning God created the heavens and the earth" (Genesis 1:1). Therefore, we must study the Holy Bible to learn, not only the truth about the end times, but also about other things that affect our lives. Our creator has given us an instruction manual about what He created and that is the Holy Bible! The Holy Bible is the infallible word of God, which He breathed through the Holy Spirit (2 Peter 1:20-21).

The Holy Bible is beneficial for sound doctrine, for rebuking and correction, and for instruction in righteousness that is from God, so that we may be perfect and equipped for God's work (2 Timothy 3:15-17). Our God is the Almighty God, the LORD, *El Shaddai*, the Source of Peace, the Ancient of Days, and the Alpha and Omega (the Beginning and the End-the First and the Last)! **"God is the only one who can tell the end from the beginning" (Isaiah 46:9-10).**

When Jesus spoke of the timing of His second coming, He said the day will close on "like a trap" (Luke 21:34). It will come "like a thief in the night", according to the Apostle Paul (1 Thessalonians 5:2). According to Jesus, no one knows the hour and the day of the Lord, not even the angels, but only the Father in heaven (Matthews 24:36). The Father, however, revealed the vision to the Son who passed it to us (the church), through the angel of the Lord to the Apostle John (Revelation 1:1).

The Day of the Lord
The Holy Bible mentions the phrase "the day of the Lord" thirty-eight times in both the Old and New Testaments. The

day of the Lord is near and will surely come as Zechariah prophesied over Jerusalem. "A day of the LORD is coming" (Zechariah 14:1). Especially for the lost, the day of the Lord will be bitter, sudden, and will come like a thief in the night (1 Thessalonians 5:3). While false teachers and their followers will say, "peace and safety", sudden destruction will come bringing great sorrow and calamities. The suddenness is described as labor pains that come unexpectedly upon a pregnant woman (1 Thessalonians 5:3). The day of the Lord will be a dark day, a day of trouble (Amos 5:18), and a day when the heavens will be destroyed by fire (2 Peter 2:10). For unbelievers, the day of the Lord is not a pleasant time. It is rather distressful and inescapable.

The prophet Ezekiel described it as "a day of clouds, a time of doom for the nations" (Ezekiel 30:3). It will be a day of judgment when everyone's works will be revealed by fire to determine whether or not they are of value (1 Corinthians 3:13). The Holy Bible encourages us not to become weary in doing good, for at the proper time or the day of the Lord we will reap a harvest (Galatians 6:7-9). Jesus is coming! "Every eye will see him, even those who pierced him" (Revelation 1:7). Scripture says Jesus will come riding a white horse (Revelation 19:11-19). He will come on the clouds of the sky, with power, and great glory (Matthew 24:30), with the angels (Matthew 25:31), and with the saints (1 Thessalonians 4:14). Christians who will be still alive at the day of the Lord and those who died in the Lord will meet the Lord in the air (1 Thessalonians 4:13-18).

When Jesus comes, the antichrist and the false prophet will be thrown into the lake of fire (Revelation 19:20) and the devil will be chained in the bottomless pit for 1,000 years

(Revelation 20:1-3). The dead in Christ, including those who died because of Jesus and for the word of God, will be resurrected and this is called *the first resurrection* (Revelation 20:4-6). The *second resurrection* will take place after the 1,000 years rule of Jesus on earth with the saints (Revelation 20:11-13). See Part 2 for the tables of the 2nd coming of Jesus, the 1st Resurrection, and the 2nd Resurrection.

The Lord, therefore, wants us to humble ourselves and seek Him during this time. Only those who are saved by the grace of God will escape the darkness of the coming days. True believers will not be surprised by the day of the Lord, as they are not in darkness (1 Thessalonians 5:4). Christians do not belong to the dark and will not be condemned. "For God did not appoint us to suffer wrath but to receive salvation through our Lord Jesus Christ." (1 Thessalonians 5:9).

According to the Apostle Peter, believers should actually "look forward to the day of the Lord and speed its coming" (2 Peter 3:12). The Holy Bible clearly recounts what will happen in the end times. Jesus sent, through His angel, "what must soon take place" (Revelation 1:1) to the Apostle John to write it to the churches.

Thank God and His Son Jesus for telling us in advance and most importantly for promising to save us from the coming wrath of God. In fact, the day of the Lord is not coming against believers but for believers! It will, however, come against those who do not believe in Jesus Christ. Believers will actually be excited, relieved, and will be at rest with the second coming of Jesus (2 Thessalonians 1:7). "And we eagerly await a Savior from there, the Lord Jesus Christ" (Philippians 3:20). We should see it as the *"blessed hope"*, as the Apostle Paul wrote to Titus, "the glorious appearing of our great God and Savior, Jesus Christ" (Titus 2:13).

Part 2:
THE SIGNS

"For many will come in my name, claiming, 'I am the Christ,' and will deceive many. You will hear of wars and rumors of wars, but see to it that you are not alarmed. Such things must happen, but the end is still to come. - - -"

(Matthew 24:5-31)

The following are *the major signs* of the day of the Lord (the last hour) that were foretold by Jesus, according to the Gospel of Matthew (Matthew 24:5-31), which will be covered in detail in this book:

1. Many will come in Jesus' name and will deceive many (v. 5). Many will turn away or fall away from faith in Jesus and will betray and hate each other (v. 10). Many false prophets or antichrists will appear and deceive many people (v. 11) (*The antichrist(s) and false prophets*). The love of most people will grow cold as a result of the increase in wickedness (v. 12).

2. You will hear of *wars* and rumors of *wars* (v. 6). Nation will rise against nation, and kingdom against kingdom (v. 7). There will be *famines and earthquakes* in various places (v. 7). There will be *great pain (great tribulation)*, beyond compare with what we have ever seen, from the beginning of the world until the end (v. 21).

3. Nations will persecute, put to death, and hate Christians because of Jesus (v. 9) *(Persecution of the church)*.

4. The Gospel of the kingdom, the Good News that God gave His Son to save the world, will be preached in the whole world as a testimony to all nations before the end will come (v. 14) *(World Wide Evangelism)*.

In addition, see below for tables of the signs and events that will occur during the day of the Lord (the last hour) including: Pre-Tribulation and Tribulations, the Great Tribulation, the 2nd Coming of Jesus, the 1st Resurrection and 2nd Resurrection, respectively:

Signs/Events before the 2nd coming	The Olivet discourse (Matthew 24)	Signs/events	Cross Reference	Seals/ trumpets/ bowls
The beginning of sorrow: False Prophets & Christ's	Mat 24:4-5	Many will come in Jesus' name claiming to be the "Christ" and they will deceive many.	Rev. 13:13-14	
Wars	Mat 24:6	You will hear of wars and rumors of wars.	Rev. 6:1-4	1st & 2nd seals
Famine, Earthquakes, Pestilence	Mat 24:7	There will be famines and earthquakes in various places.	Rev. 6:5-8, 6:12	3rd, 4th, & 6th seals
Satan cast down to earth		And there was war in heaven. Michael and his angels fought against the dragon. The great dragon (that ancient serpent called the devil, or Satan, who leads the whole world astray) was hurled down to the earth, and his angels with him.	Rev 12:7-17	
Tribulations (first 3½ years of the 70th week): Persecution	Mat 24:9	Christians will be handed over to be persecuted, put to death, and will be hated by all nations because of Jesus.	Rev. 6:9, 12:17	5th seal
Apostasy, false prophets, increased wickedness	Mat 24:10-12	At that time many will turn away from the faith (apostasy). Many false prophets will appear and deceive many people. Increased wickedness and the love of most will grow cold.	Rev. 13:11-18	
The Gospel is preached world wide	Mat 24:13-14	The Gospel will be preached in the whole world as a testimony to all nations.	Mark 13:10	

(Table of the Pre-Tribulation and Tribulations)

Signs/Events before the 2nd coming	The Olivet discourse (Matthew 24)	Signs/events	Cross Reference
Great tribulation (last 3½ years of the 70th week): Jerusalem & the Temple's desolation	Mat 24:2 , Mat 24:15-22,	Jesus said, "I tell you the truth, not one stone here will be left on another; everyone will be thrown down." (Mat. 24:2). "When you see Jerusalem being surrounded by armies, you will know that its desolation is near (Luke 21:20). "The abomination that causes desolation" will be standing in the holy place (Mat 24:15).	Daniel 9:26-27, Luke 21:20-24
Israel to flee		Israel will flee to the mountains (Mat 24:16).	
Great tribulation/ length		That day will be dreadful and there will be great distress. The days will be shortened for the sake of the elect (Mat 24:21-22).	Rev. 11:3, 12:6, 12:14, 13:5,
False Christs and False Prophets (Signs and wonders)	Mat 24:23-26,	The secret power of lawlessness (antichrists (1 John 2:18)) is already at work (2 Th. 2:7) and will perform great signs and miracles to deceive even the elect (Mat 24:23-26). The antichrist will be coming in accordance with the work of Satan displayed in all kinds of counterfeit miracles, signs and wonders, and in every sort of evil (2 Th. 2:9-10). The antichrist will oppose and exalt himself over everything that is called God or is worshiped, so that he sets himself up in God's temple, proclaiming himself to be God (2 Th. 2:4).	Rev. 13:13-14, 1 John 2:18, 2 Th. 2:4-10

(Table of the Great Tribulation)

Signs/Events of the 2nd coming	The Olivet discourse (Matthew 24)	Signs/events	Cross Reference	Seals/ trumpets/ bowls
2nd coming/ revelation: Signs in heavens	Mat 24:27 Mat 24:29	As lightning comes from the east *is visible* even in the west, so will be the coming of the Son of Man. *"Immediately after the distress of those days* "the sun will be darkened, and the moon will not give its light; the stars will fall from the sky, and the heavenly bodies will be shaken.'	Rev. 6:12-14, 8:12, 16:8-11	6th seal, 1st to 4th trumpets, 1st to 5th bowl judgments
2nd coming	Mat 24:30	"At that time the sign of the Son of Man will appear in the sky and all the nations of the earth will mourn. *They will see the Son of Man coming* on the clouds of the sky, with power and great glory.	Luke 21:27 Rev. 19:11-16	
Armageddon- (the final conflict between Christ and antichrist).		The man (antichrist) is doomed for destruction (2 Th. 2:3). The beast (antichrist), the kings of the earth and their armies gathered together to make war against the rider on the horse (Jesus) and His army (the angels) -Rev 16:16. Then the beast (antichrist) was captured, and with him the false prophet and were thrown alive into the lake of fire (Rev. 19:19-20). Jesus will overthrow *the lawless one* with the breath of His mouth and destroy by the splendor of His coming (2 Th. 2:8).	Rev. 16:16, 19:11-21, 2 Th. 2:3, 8	6th & 7th bowl judgments
Satan chained for 1,000 years		Satan chained for 1,000 years (Rev. 20:1-3).	Rev. 20:1-3	

(Table of the 2nd coming of Jesus)

Signs/Events of the 2nd coming	The Olivet discourse (Matthew 24)	Signs/events	Cross Reference	Seals/ trumpets / bowls
Resurrection - *(A rising again; a return from death to life)* & Rapture *(in Latin is rapiemur (harpazó in Greek) meaning to seize, catch up, snatch away):*	Mat 24:31	And He will send His angels *with a loud trumpet call,* and they will gather *His elect* from the four winds, from one end of the heavens to the other (Mat. 24:31). Jesus comes with a loud command, with the voice of the archangel, and with (at) the trumpet (the 7th trumpet- Rev. 11:15) call of God (1Th 4:16), in a flash, in a twinkling of an eye (1 Cor. 15:52).	Rev. 6:9, 11:15-18, 20:4-6; 1 Th 4:14-17; 1 Cor. 15:51-52; John 5:29; Dan. 12:2; Acts 24:15.	7th trumpet, 5th seal
1st Resurrection (of the righteous (saints) & the martyrs		The saints (the righteous) (John 5:29; Dan. 12:2; & Acts 24:15.) including the tribulation saints (Rev. 6:9) will be raised from the dead first (*the 1st resurrection-* Rev 20:4-6). God will bring with Jesus the saints (who died in him) (1 Th 4:14). Those alive at the time of Jesus' 2nd coming will not precede those that are *dead in Christ* (1 Th 4:15).		
Rapture		Those alive will be *caught up (& changed)* to meet Jesus in the air with the resurrected saints (1 Th 4:17).		
The Millennial Kingdom		The saints resurrected and changed (raptured) will reign and live, for 1,000 years, with Jesus (Rev. 20:6).		
Satan's final destiny		Satan will be released after the 1,000 years is over and he will gather Gog Magog for war. Gog Magog will be destroyed by fire and Satan will be thrown into the lake of fire (Rev. 20:7-10).	Rev. 20:7-10, Ezekiel 38:1-23	

(Table of the 1st Resurrection)

14

Signs/Events of the 2nd coming	Matthew 25	Signs/events	Cross Reference
2nd (general) Resurrection	Mat 25:31-32 Mat 25:41 Mat 25:46	The dead rose to life and were judged. Each person was judged according to what he had done (Rev. 20:12-13). "Those who committed the evil deeds to a resurrection of judgment." (John 5:29). (Resurrection of the wicked- Acts 24:15). The second and last death is the throwing of death and Hades into the lake of fire (Rev. 20:14). (The last enemy (death) is destroyed- (1 Corinthians 15:26). Finally the unsaved, whose names are not found in the book of life, are thrown into the lake of fire (Rev. 20:15).	Rev. 20:11-15; 1 Cor. 15:26; John 5:29; Dan. 12:2; Acts 24:15.

(Table of the 2nd Resurrection)

CHAPTER 2:
THE ANTICHRIST(S)

"… the antichrist is coming, even now many antichrists have come…"
(1 John 2:18)

Who is the Antichrist?

The word *"antichrist"*, in Greek, is *"antichristos"*. It means the adversary of the Messiah or one who opposes Christ. The word *"antichrist"* is mentioned in the Holy Bible only four times, all in the New Testament–three times in the 1st Epistle of John and once in the 2nd Epistle of John. The antichrist is a man to be used by the devil, a man of lawlessness, and a man of sin or inequity. The antichrist is also called the "son of perdition". It means destruction and is described by the Apostle Paul as *"the lawless one"*.

Deceptive

The antichrist is a false Christ who will deceive many by claiming that he is the Messiah. He will oppose Jesus and His people, and declares himself to be God. In reality he is an enemy or opponent of Jesus who wants to be exulted above all that is called God or that is worshipped as God (2 Thessalonians 2:3). Those who believe the lies of the antichrist will perish because they are following destruction, and have not received the true Gospel and tasted the love of our Lord Jesus Christ. Jesus will punish unbelievers with eternal penalty (2 Thessalonians 1:8-9).

Deceitful

The antichrist is called a liar with the power of Satan, according to 2 Thessalonians 2:9-10 and those like him are called antichrists. Antichrists deny God and the truth that Jesus is the Christ and the Son of God (1 John 2:22). Those who deny the existence of God, the creator of all—also called "atheists" are therefore antichrists. For example, John 1:14 says, "the Word became flesh and made his dwelling among us" and the prophet Isaiah also foretold that a virgin would have a child and call Him Emmanuel, which is translated, "God with us" (Isaiah 7:14). This prophecy was fulfilled when Jesus was born (Matthew 1:23). Antichrists, however, deny the fulfillment and validity of this prophecy.

Anyone who does not acknowledge and believe that Jesus came in the flesh (2 John 1:7 & 1 John 4:3), and that Jesus died on the cross is following the spirit of the antichrist. The Apostle Paul wrote to Timothy that the great mystery of the Christian faith is that Jesus "appeared in a body" (1Timothy 3:16). Some claimed Jesus was John the Baptist, including King Herod (Mark 6:16), and others said Elijah. Some have believed this because Elijah was taken up to heaven alive by God and that he will return before the second coming of Jesus. It also signifies that John the Baptist came in the spirit of Elijah. Antichrists reject the appearing of Jesus in a physical body.

Still others thought Jesus was Jeremiah, or one of the other prophets (Matthew 16:14). All such notions were from the flesh and not from God. God wants us to know and believe that Jesus is the Son of God. "But these are written that you may believe that Jesus is the Christ, the Son of God, and that by believing you may have life in his name." (John 20:31). Antichrists deceive others by confusing them regarding the true identity of Jesus.

The Beast of Daniel 7

The prophet Daniel saw four beasts in a vision and the fourth beast he saw was a fourth kingdom (Daniel 7:7). This kingdom will devour the whole earth and ten kings will come out of it. After them another king (the little horn) will arise.

This new king will destroy three of the ten kings, will speak against the Most High, and oppresses the saints (representing Israel & believers) for three and a half years. The remaining seven kings will give their power to the beast (Revelation 17:13). Therefore, this new and eighth king that is different from the other kings is the antichrist (Revelation 17:11-12).

The Beast of Revelation 13

The beast of Revelation 13 also represents the antichrist (Revelation 13:1-5). Although the beast is not a lion he looks like a lion. The real lion is the Lion of the tribe of Judah and the Root of David-Jesus Christ! The antichrist deceives others by claiming that he is the savior of the world and he yearns to be worshipped as God. According to Revelation 13:8, those who worship him are the inhabitants of the earth who are unbelievers and whose names have not been recorded in the Lamb's Book of Life. The number 666 is the mark of the beast and it will be visible on the foreheads or right arms of those who worship the beast.

The beast will have ten horns or thrones and seven heads. The ten horns represent the ten kings who will rule on earth (Daniel 7:23). These are unbelieving and liberal kings who hate anything that is God's. The antichrist also boasts and blasphemes against God and His people (Revelation 13:5-6). The antichrist and anyone who is possessed by the spirit of the antichrist (1 John 4:3) are against the church of God and Christians.

Blasphemy

Satan likes to copy God or what God does. However, he does it in the exact opposite way out of rebellion and hatred. For example, Satan wants to keep people captive and destroy them, while God wants people to be set free to worship Him. Satan said, "I will make myself like the Most High" (Isaiah 14:14). Likewise, the antichrist will blaspheme and proclaim himself to be God (2 Thessalonians 2:4) and thereby imitates Satan.

Transfer of Power

In the Book of Exodus, God told Moses to go to Egypt and tell Pharaoh to let the Israelites go free. When Moses said, "I cannot speak eloquently," God gave Aaron to Moses. God was then speaking to Moses and Moses speaks to Aaron so that Aaron in turn speaks to the Pharaoh (Exodus 6:10-16). Likewise, in the end times, the transfer of chain of power or authority is from Satan (the dragon) to the antichrist (the beast) (Revelation 13:2), and then from the antichrist to the false prophet (Revelation 13:12).

The Prophecy-The Desolation of the Temple of God and the City of Jerusalem

The prophecy of the destruction of the temple and the city of Jerusalem was first spoken by the prophet Daniel. "Know and understand this: From the issuing of the decree to restore and rebuild Jerusalem until the Anointed One, the ruler, comes, there will be seven 'sevens' and sixty-two 'sevens.' It will be rebuilt with streets and a trench, but in times of trouble. After the sixty-two 'sevens,' the Anointed One will be cut off and will have nothing. The people of the ruler who will come will destroy the city and the sanctuary. **The end will come like a flood: War will continue until the end, and desolations have been decreed.**

He will confirm a covenant with many for one 'seven'. In the middle of the 'seven' he will put an end to sacrifice and offering. And on a wing [of the temple] he will set up an abomination that causes desolation, until the end that is decreed is poured out on him" (Daniel 9:25-27). Jesus also foretold the destruction of the temple in Matthew 24:1-2.

The Seventy "Sevens" or "Weeks"-Daniel's first 69 "Weeks"

There were seventy "sevens" or "weeks" (with each "week" having seven years) decreed about the people of Israel and the city of Jerusalem, according to the angel Gabriel who gave the message to Daniel (Daniel 9:24).

The city of Jerusalem and the temple of God had already been destroyed at the time the Israelites were delivered into Babylonian captivity in 609 B.C., because of sin and rebellion. The two major events that occurred during the first 69 "weeks", equating in total to 483 years include: the rebuilding of Jerusalem (the city with its temple and walls during the time of Ezra and Nehemiah), and the birth of Jesus.

The end of the 69th "week" denotes the time of Jesus' crucifixion (around 33A.D.). Following the crucifixion of Jesus, the temple that existed at the time of Jesus (also called the "Herod's Temple") and the city of Jerusalem were destroyed by the Romans some 37 years later, in A.D. 70.

The Prophecy- "The End Will Come" (The Gap Between Daniel's 69th and 70th "Week")

After the 69th "week", the end will come like a flood and then there will remain only one final period of seven years, called Daniel's 70th "week" (Daniel 9:26-27). The vision

Daniel saw was a vision about the end times, according to the angel Gabriel (Daniel 8:17). This vision also referred to the things that **"will happen later in the time of wrath"** (Daniel 8:19), and the "distant future" (Daniel 8:26). There is therefore a time gap between Daniel's 69th and 70th "week".

The Coming of the Antichrist

The antichrist is working behind the scene "in secret", according to the Apostle Paul (2 Thessalonians 2:7). However, the antichrist will not be revealed until the appointed time, even if his spirit is already working (1 John 2:18). The end does not come until the antichrist is revealed first. He will appear at the end of this present age.

Therefore, the arrival of the antichrist precedes the second coming of Jesus (2 Thessalonians 2:3). The prophet Daniel also wrote about the coming of the antichrist in Daniel Chapter 9. He comes after the Messiah (the true Christ) is crucified and died, resurrected, and ascended to the heavens (cutoff) (Daniel 9:26). Antichrists and their spirits are alive and actively work in secret. It is, therefore, foolishness to think they are not alive and working today.

The Seventy "Sevens" or "Weeks"-Daniel's 70th "Week"

The 70th "week" is the last seven years the antichrist will be ruling on earth. The desolation, also called the time of God's wrath, will be poured upon the antichrist at the end of the last seven year (Daniel's 70th "week"). It therefore did not happen in A.D. 70 and is referring to a future date. Some people believe the day of the Lord had already come, like the Thessalonians. However, the Holy Bible attributes the time of God's wrath at the sounding of the 7th trumpet, to a future date, as we read Revelation 11:18, "And your wrath has come. The time has come for judging the dead and for rewarding your servants the prophets and your saints."

The Prophecy- The Desecration of the Temple of God

The antichrist replaces the true worship of God just before the second coming of Jesus. He exalts himself as God and desecrates the temple of God (2 Thessalonians 2:2-4). When the antichrist, the ruler of the people, comes, he is going to make a covenant with many for seven years (Daniel's 70th "week"). However, three and a half years into this last seven years, he will stop the sacrifice and the offering in the temple, and display an idol and image of a false god in the temple of God (Daniel 9:27 and 11:31). This temple is the one that will have to be rebuilt since Jesus Himself indicated that the prophecy was not yet fulfilled (Mark 13:14 and Matthew 24:15).

The Apostle Paul also noted the desecration of the temple of God, when writing to the Thessalonians about the **coming of the day of the Lord,** which clearly did not point to the past destruction of the "Herod's temple" in A.D. 70 (2 Thessalonians 2:1-4). Finally, "from the time that the daily sacrifice is abolished and the abomination that causes desolation is set up, there will be 1,290 days" (Daniel 12:11). This describes the last three and a half years of the last seven years of Daniel's 70th "week".

The Antichrist Destroyed

The antichrist will be captured alive and thrown into the lake of fire. At the appointed time, Jesus will finally destroy the antichrist by His breath, when He comes in blazing fire and with His powerful angels (2 Thessalonians 2:8). The double edged sword coming out of Jesus' mouth (Revelation 19:15-20) refers to the word of God. When Jesus comes back, He will set up an everlasting kingdom. The Holy Bible says "the thief comes only to steal and kill and destroy; I have come that they may have life, and have it to the full" (John 10:10). Jesus was sent by God to save the world while the antichrist will be sent by the devil to attack and destroy the saints of God. Jesus is also the one "who rescues us from the coming wrath" (1 Thessalonians 1:10). Hallelujah! See Part 2 for the tables of the Pre-Tribulation and Tribulations and the Great Tribulation.

In conclusion, Jesus warned us in advance so that we may not be deceived by the antichrists of our time. So Christians should watch for the day of the Lord (the last hour) and discern the time! It is because of the anointing each one of us has received from God and through the Holy Spirit that we can discern antichrists of our time, both in the church and in the world. Yes, we can overcome the antichrists of our time, as the Holy Bible says, "the one who is in you is greater than the one who is in the world." (1 John 4:4).

CHAPTER 3:
FALSE CHRISTS AND PROPHETS

"For false Christs and false prophets will appear and perform great signs and miracles to deceive even the elect—if that were possible."
(Matthew 24:24)

False Christs and False Prophets

The phrase "false Christs" is mentioned twice, while the phrase "false prophets" is mentioned twelve times in the Holy Bible. Jesus foretold the rise of false Christs in the Gospels, which is one of the signs of the last hour (Matthew 24:24 & Mark 13:22). These false Christs and prophets will come in Jesus' name and deceive many by performing miraculous signs that are actually from the devil.

According to the Apostle Peter, many false prophets and teachers or prophets with antichrist spirits will appear to deceive many with their teachings. "They will secretly introduce destructive heresies, even denying the sovereign Lord." (2 Peter 2:1). False prophets and teachers lead individuals, as well as congregations, astray by their error and false teaching. They create confusion by perverting the true Gospel of Christ (Galatians 1:7). This is evidenced by the many divisions we see in churches today. The Apostle Peter also warns that scoffers will mock by following their own evil desires, and are reserved for punishment at the day of judgment (2 Peter 3:3-7).

In addition, the Apostle John warned that many of these false prophets had already gone out into the world (1 John 4:1). The Apostle Paul also called these false prophets, "false apostles" and "deceitful workmen" (2 Corinthians 11:13). The antichrist spirit is working in false Christs and false prophets and teachers to deceive many. The spirit of the antichrist is characterized by the spirit of unbelief that denies and rejects Jesus and all that is called and worshipped as God as well as by the spirit of apostasy; and the spirit of falling away and wickedness.

The word *"apostasy"* or *"apostasia"*, in Greek, is defined as *"rebellion, defection, revolt, or falling away"* (2 Thessalonians 2:3). The Apostle Paul also defined apostasy to mean *"to depart from the faith"* (1st Timothy 4:1). Apostasy signifies forsaking the true faith, and blaspheming against the Holy Spirit. False teachers and prophets and false Christs have the following four main characteristics, as depicted by the Apostle Paul in 1st Timothy 6:3-5:

1. <u>Teach False Doctrines</u>

These are the ones who teach false doctrines about our Lord Jesus Christ and are therefore false teachers. They deceive people with their teachings. They also disagree with the word of God, with sound doctrine, and with godly teaching.

2. <u>Confuse and deceive</u>

They are the ones who understand nothing and lack the truth. The spirit of unbelief is the idea that there are other ways of being saved than through Jesus. For example, the New Age Movement opposes Christianity and is hostile to Christians. It rejects and denies the view that there is only one God who is revealed in the person of Jesus Christ.

It tries to distort and deny the true identity of Jesus as the only savior, and promotes many other false gods in His place. It holds a pagan world view that is crafted by that old serpent, the devil. It encourages sin and even backs it up with research done by its members. It promotes the idea that society would be better off if there were no Christianity. However, Scriptures say the universe is created by its creator, God, and He will punish those opposing Him in due time!

3. **Controversial and Wicked**

They are those that are controversial, quarrelsome, envious, malicious, suspicious, and have corrupt minds. The Apostle Paul wrote, "quarreling about words; it is of no value, and only ruins those who listen" (2 Timothy 2:14). Therefore, we should not listen or follow false prophets.

4. **Opportunist**

They are opportunists who think godliness is merely a means to financial gain. The Apostle Peter called these teachers abusive and liars (2 Peter 2:3). Jude also called these false teachers immoral and godless men, shepherds who feed only themselves, and those that deny Jesus Christ, our only Sovereign and Lord (Jude 1:4 and 1:12).

The False Prophet

The false prophet is mentioned only four times in the Book of Revelation. The second beast in Revelation 13:11 is the false prophet who looks like Jesus but speaks like a dragon. But behind his true identity is the devil himself. He uses the antichrist's authority and power to deceive people and causing them to worship the antichrist. He will also order them to setup and worship the image of the antichrist and to receive the mark of the beast. As a result, many will turn away (fall away) from the faith of believing in Jesus and "will betray and hate each other" (Matthew 24:10). The false prophet is the man who will be working hand in hand with the antichrist to perform miraculous signs on behalf of the antichrist or the beast (Revelation 19:20). The purpose of the miraculous signs and wonders is to gather the kings of the whole world for battle on the day of the Lord

(Revelation 16:14), and to deceive those who received the mark of the beast (the number 666) to worship the image of the antichrist. Those miracles occur by the power of the devil, the antichrist, and the false prophet (Revelation 16:13).

The False Prophet Destroyed

The false prophet and the antichrist will be captured alive and thrown into the lake of fire (Revelation 19:19-20). See Part 2 for the tables of the Pre-Tribulation and Tribulations and the Great Tribulation. In conclusion, we should not be deceived by false prophets and false Christs. Like the Bereans of Acts 17:11, we must therefore examine and study the word of God to be able to discern when such false teachers and prophets and false Christs are in error.

CHAPTER 4:
WARS, FAMINE AND EARTHQUAKES, AND GREAT TRIBULATION

"When you hear of wars and rumors of wars, do not be alarmed. Such things must happen, but the end is still to come. Nation will rise against nation and kingdom against kingdom. There will be earthquakes in various places, and famines. These are the beginning of birth pains."
(Mark 13:7-8)

"... those will be days of distress unequaled from the beginning, when God created the world, until now—and never to be equaled again."
(Mark 13:19)

Wars

We live in times of war. Wars and rumors of wars will continue and increase at an alarming rate till Jesus returns. According to the Apostle John, peace will be taken from the earth when the second seal is opened (Revelation 6:3-4). The prophet Daniel was also told by the angel Gabriel that wars will continue like a flood to the end (Daniel 9:26). For instance, let's see the causalities and cost of the past few major wars and what the last two wars will be like:

World War I and II

An estimated 11 million and 59 million people were killed during World War I and II, respectively. The estimated costs of these two wars were $196.5 billion and $2,091.3 billion, respectively (Where can I see World War 1, World War 2, and World War 3 Statistics? Three World War Statistics Compared, 2009).

The Iraq War

Civilian casualties of the Iraq War are estimated to be over 100,000. In addition, as of October, 2010, 4,430 US Soldiers were killed while 31,929 were seriously wounded. As a result of the Iraq war, the U.S. approved and spent approximately $900 billion through October 2010, according to About.com (White, 2010).

The Last Two Wars

The final two wars will be the Armageddon war and the war with the Gog and Magog. The Armageddon war is the final conflict between Christ and the antichrist. The antichrist and the kings of the earth and their armies will gather together to make war against the rider on the horse (Jesus) and His army (the angels) (Revelation 16:16).

The antichrist is doomed to destruction (2 Thessalonians 2:3). Jesus will overthrow the lawless one or the antichrist with the breath of His mouth and destroy him by the splendor of His coming (2 Thessalonians 2:8). The beast or antichrist will be captured, and with him the false prophet and will be thrown alive into the lake of fire.

The last major war will be the war with Gog and Magog. After the end of 1,000 years of Jesus' rule on earth (the millennial reign), Satan will be released and will then gather Gog and Magog for war. Finally, Gog and Magog will be destroyed by fire, as it was foretold by the prophet Ezekiel in 585 B.C., and Satan will be thrown into the lake of fire (Revelation 20:7-10). See Part 2 for the tables of the 2nd Coming of Jesus and the 1st Resurrection.

Famine

Global hunger or famine is one of the major human crises of our time. Again the Holy Bible clearly warns beforehand of the occurrence of famine. "When the Lamb opened the third seal, I heard the third living creature say, "Come!" I looked, and there before me was a black horse! Its rider was holding a pair of scales in his hand. Then I heard what sounded like a voice among the four living creatures, saying, "A quart of wheat for a day's wages, and three quarts of barley for a day's wages, and do not damage the oil and the wine!" (Revelation 6:5-6). Jesus showed the Apostle John what will occur just before His return regarding hunger and famine and worldwide economic crises.

The following is a report from the World Food Program on world hunger titled "***GLOBAL HUNGER***":

- "925 million people do not have enough to eat - more than the populations of USA, Canada and the European Union; *(Source: FAO news release, 14 September 2010)*
- 98 percent of the world's hungry live in developing countries; *(Source: FAO news release, 2010)*
- Asia and the Pacific region is home to over half the world's population and nearly two thirds of the world's hungry people; *(Source: FAO news release, 2010)*
- Women make up a little over half of the world's population, but they account for over 60 percent of the world's hungry. *(Source: Strengthening efforts to eradicate hunger..., ECOSOC, 2007)*
- 65 percent of the world's hungry live in only seven countries: India, China, the Democratic Republic of Congo, Bangladesh, Indonesia, Pakistan and Ethiopia. *(Source: FAO news release, 2010)*" (Hunger Stats, 2010).

Earthquakes

Earthquakes are increasing and the causalities are unimaginable in terms of loss of life and cost of property damages. "There was a great earthquake; and the sun became black as sackcloth of hair, and the moon became as blood." (Revelation 6:12). Jesus showed the Apostle John what happens before His return, when the sixth seal is opened.

The United States Geological Survey tracks, monitors, and researches earthquakes and the effects of earthquake hazards. It also reports the number of deaths, the magnitude of earthquakes, and the frequency of earthquake occurrences. See the following two charts for details:

Frequency of Occurrence of Earthquake (United States Geological Survey, 2010)

Magnitude Average	Annually
8 and higher	1 [1]
7 - 7.9	15 [2]
6 - 6.9	134 [2]
5 - 5.9	1319 [2]
4 - 4.9 (estimated)	13,000
3 - 3.9 (estimated)	130,000
2 - 2.9 (estimated)	1,300,000

[1] Based on observations since 1900.
[2] Based on observations since 1990.

Number of Earthquakes Worldwide for years 2000 to 2010
(United States Geological Survey, 2010)

Magnitude	2000	2001	2002	2003	2004	2005	2006	2007	2008	2009	2010*
8.0–9.9	1	1	0	1	2	1	1	4	0	1	1
7.0–7.9	14	15	13	14	14	10	10	14	12	16	19
6.0–6.9	146	121	127	140	141	140	142	178	168	142	133
5.0–5.9	1,344	1,224	1,201	1,203	1,515	1,693	1,712	2,074	1,768	1,855	1,519
4.0–4.9	8,008	7,991	8,541	8,462	10,888	13,917	12,838	12,078	12,291	6,830	7,819
3.0–3.9	4,827	6,266	7,068	7,624	7,932	9,191	9,990	9,889	11,735	2,903	3,510
2.0–2.9	3,765	4,164	6,419	7,727	6,316	4,636	4,027	3,597	3,860	3,013	3,451
1.0–1.9	1,026	944	1,137	2,506	1,344	26	18	42	21	26	23
0.1–0.9	5	1	10	134	103	0	2	2	0	1	0
No magnitude	3,120	2,807	2,938	3,608	2,939	864	828	1,807	1,922	18	25
Total	22,256	23,534	27,454	31,419	31,194	30,478	29,568	29,685	31,777	14,805	16,500
Estimated deaths	231	21,357	1,685	33,819	228,802	88,003	6,605	712	88,011	1,787	226,623

* As of November 1, 2010.

In 2010, two major earthquakes occurred in Haiti and Chile. The estimated cost for the Haitian earthquake could be $13 billion dollars (with a death toll estimated at 250,000) while the Chile earthquake could end up costing more than $30 billion dollars. In addition, a number of other earthquakes were happening frequently after these two major earthquakes in 2010. In fact, a total of 61 major earthquakes occurred up to November 3, 2010, which is an average of 6 earthquakes per month.

Tribulations or Perilous Times

The Apostle Paul's second letter to Timothy describes in detail what happens in the end times. "But mark this: There will be terrible times in the last days. People will be lovers of themselves, lovers of money, boastful, proud, abusive, disobedient to their parents, ungrateful, unholy, without love, unforgiving, slanderous, without self-control, brutal, not lovers of the good, treacherous, rash, conceited, lovers of pleasure rather than lovers of God—having a form of godliness but denying its power. Have nothing to do with them." (2 Timothy 3:1-5).

Selfishness and Unloving

Increased self-love indicates the declining morality and increased wickedness of the society in which we live today. Our society is so selfish and confused that we no longer have compassion for our fellow human beings, but reserve kindness for mere animals and nature, and call it *"humane."* We have ignored the suffering of other human beings, our brothers and sisters, who are in distress. This is the result of being unthankful and selfishness. The love of money is demonstrated in the decline of charity and compassion toward starving people. Nowadays, people would rather donate money to save animals rather than to save the lives of starving children in developing nations.

Many people nowadays care more about animals than their neighbors or friends. Many liberal organizations have also organized to ban medical research and testing on animals. They want to prohibit the use of animal skins or eating meat in the name of liberalism and vegetarianism. The antichrist spirit is responsible for liberalism and secularism.

At the same time, we have failed to speak up for or to protect millions of people in Darfur (Sudan), Haiti, and around the world where Christians are persecuted for the name of Jesus. Rather than majoring on God's most precious creations, the human beings who are created in the image of God, our society is focused on the minor things.

Just as Jesus was depicted as the humble and suffering servant in the Gospel of Mark, we must learn to humble ourselves and learn to serve and love others. We need to be willing to go the extra mile with friends and the people around us. Jesus warned that the love of many would grow cold in the end times (Matthew 24:12).

Sadly, it is not any more unusual for parents to kill their children, for children to kill their parents and for husbands and wives to kill each other. "The thief comes only to steal and kill and destroy" (John 10:10). Since Satan could not target God Himself, he set his sights on those God loves and their families. As a result, they have suffered tremendously due to the influence of secular thinking and laws that hinder the practice of Christianity. People are advocating different things that are not in line with the word of God. The antichrist spirit has used those in power to pass laws that do not line up with God's word, making it difficult for Christians to express their personal love for God in public without negative repercussions.

Lovers of Money

The love of money does not require much explanation as money is a necessity in our everyday lives and is universally attractive to everyone. It causes grief to those that are pursuing it and could not satisfy themselves with it. People kill, steal, and cause great harm to others for money. The crime rate for robbing banks and people is increasing. The US dollar is called by many people the "Almighty Dollar", an example of an idol. Forfeiting our souls and gaining the things this world has to offer is a very great loss, and results in eternal death and separation from God.

Pride and Boasting

Pride and boasting are rebellion that caused the casting of the devil from the heavens. Isaiah 14:13-15 says: "You said in your heart, "I will ascend to heaven; I will raise my throne above the stars of God; I will sit enthroned on the mount of assembly, on the utmost heights of the sacred mountain. I will ascend above the tops of the clouds; I will make myself like the Most High." But you are brought down to the grave, to the depths of the pit". Nothing will destroy our walk with God faster than pride and a boastful spirit. God cannot use those who are full of themselves. His anointing can only flow freely through a humble spirit.

Blasphemy

Blasphemy is another sign of perilous times in which we live. Blasphemers treat God and the things of God with great disrespect and hate those who love Him. They despise holiness, and pervert the word of God, denying its power. Blasphemy is a spirit of the antichrist that is against God and the saints.

For example, the antichrist will be revealed to blaspheme God and the saints. Revelation 13:5-6 says: "The beast was given a mouth to utter proud words and blasphemies and to exercise his authority for forty-two months. He opened his mouth to blaspheme God and to slander his name and his dwelling place and those who live in heaven".

Disobedient to Parents

It is not uncommon in our day to see children disobeying their parents. This is due to the increased wickedness and the influence of the spirit of the air or prince of the power of the air (Ephesians 2:1-3). Disciplining children is now seen by many as a crime, but the Holy Bible says, "Do not withhold discipline from a child; if you punish him with the rod, he will not die. Punish him with the rod and save his soul from death." (Proverbs 23:13-14). We need to train our children to be godly, to respect and fear God, and use loving discipline to help them become wise and self-disciplined.

Unthankful

Not being thankful is a sign of end times. Thanking God for His blessings is very important for we are bought with the blood of Jesus Christ. We are indebted to Jesus. In fact, as believers we should be the most grateful people on earth. So, when we feel like complaining we should take our needs to the Lord, and thank Him for the answers we have yet to see, knowing they are already on the way.

The Holy Bible says, "Give thanks in all circumstances, for this is God's will for you in Christ Jesus." (1 Thessalonians 5:18). However, people everywhere are heard complaining and being unthankful. People complain when it is raining, snowing, or sunny. People also complain when living in their native land as well as abroad.

The American holiday known as Thanksgiving began as a celebration of thankfulness to God, but even that has become distorted to mean a time to overindulge and watch football games. We need to get back to the basics of thanksgiving, and thank God in everything.

Unholy

Morality has declined to its lowest point since the beginning of time. Ungodliness has permeated not only the secular media but also extends to the church of Jesus Christ. Holiness is seen as a thing of the past and for the uncivilized or uneducated, when the truth is, God has never changed His position on the subject. Holiness is God's character. Those who love God and walk in holiness are considered "out of their minds" by those around them. 1 Peter 1:16 says we are to be sanctified or set apart to God.

Nowadays, we see every trace of God being removed from our lives, from the courthouse to our dollar bills, as if we owe Him nothing. The New Age Movement has tried to replace God from school systems and work places with yoga and eastern mysticism. Churches that used to exalt Jesus are now asking us to accept homosexuality as "normal" when God says He despises such behavior. Pastors were heard saying they were having a "holy moment" when voting on accepting homosexuality in the church, and as a result dividing their church because of their personal agendas.

The church has accepted a lie in place of the truth. Romans 1:25 says: "They exchanged the truth of God for a lie". The truth is that these "churches" are not really churches at all. This is because they refused to give God His rightful place and did not exalt Him or His word. These "churches" do not believe in Jesus and do not want to even hear His name mentioned. Rather, these "churches" exalt personal experience, conscience, and human reasoning.

They exalt men rather than God, and tickle the ears of listeners instead of giving the unvarnished truth of the Gospel and warning men of the judgment to come. I wonder what is sung, worshiped, called upon, or prayed to in those "churches" that do not give final authority to the word of God! They are synagogues of Satan (Revelation 2:9) and demonic (Psalms 96:5).

The church is the house of God and the place of worship and prayer. It is to be a place that welcomes unbelievers, inviting them to come and be transformed. The church is not a place custom made for those who refuse the message of salvation. Sinners are not a special class, an "endangered species", to be protected by the government or a liberal religion. All sinners just need Jesus to be saved and to have eternal life, like everyone else. Jesus died for all humanity. Unbelievers are already in sins and they remain under God's angry judgment. When Jesus comes, He will say to unbelievers and those who deny the truth, "I never knew you"!

God created Adam and Eve in His image and He created them male and female (Genesis 1:27) intending for the union of one man and one woman who were faithful to each other. Nowhere do Scriptures allow for a child to have two mothers or two fathers. No matter what we teach in schools or the secular media, a child only has one mothers and fathers as biological parents. The truth does not change just because we say it is so. We had better return to our roots, the pure word of God and His holiness. If we accept such lies from the father of lies himself, the Devil, we will pay for it forever in hell.

In addition, in some workplaces, Christian employees have to choose between losing their jobs and accepting what goes against their beliefs. For example, during Christmas time, employees are forced by employers to greet customers with "Seasons greetings" or "Happy holidays" rather than "Merry Christmas".

Many people prefer to hear "thank you" rather than the words, "God bless you." Others will accept "God bless you," as long as the name of Jesus is not mentioned. Wickedness is now openly visible and without shame in the society in which we live. These days, people actually look forward to hearing bad news, because good news no longer holds their interest. Many would prefer not to hear how the Lord is working around the world. What a generation and time! "Woe to those who call evil good and good evil... " (Isaiah 5:20).

The Apostle Paul wrote to the Romans about those who not only continue to do unholy things, but also about those who approve others who practice them (Romans 1:32). There is a season for everything (Ecclesiastes 3:1-8). There is a season for sowing and reaping. God cannot be mocked and if we do not grow weary, we will reap what we have sown (Galatians 6:7-9). Every one of us will give an account to Jesus for what we have done for "man is destined to die once, and after that to face judgment" (Hebrews 9:27).

Unforgiving

The spirit of not forgiving is on the rise and is even infiltrating churches. Divisions in the church are also increasing. The Apostle Paul wrote to the church in Corinth that their church was defeated because of divisions. "The very fact that you have lawsuits among you means you have been completely defeated already." (1 Corinthians 6:7).

Many unbelievers have left churches because of hurts and divisions in the church. This is one reason why some refuse invitations to attend church anywhere. May God help those who serve in the church! The church is now a place for hypocrites and those who do not have the patience to help those hypocrites to recover, and help them turn to the Lord.

The church must welcome and extend love to everyone and it has the duty to teach the truth that actually changes hearts, resolves issues, and encourages people to live righteously in this present evil world. "Those who are wise will shine like the brightness of the heavens, and those who lead many to righteousness, like the stars forever and ever." (Daniel 12:3).

Slanderers

Slanderers are those who deny the truth of Scriptures and reject the person of Jesus Christ. For example, slanderers hide the real story of Christmas from the public and confuse those who have no idea about Christianity so that they remain unaware of the truth. Jesus was born over 2,000 years ago, and since then we have been blessed to live in times of grace—the New Testament period.

However, the good news of Christ's birth has been replaced by fictional stories of Santa Claus and by overspending on frivolous gifts, completely ignoring the point, that Jesus was the best gift of all! Our early church fathers worshipped God with psalms because they understood the meaning of God's grace and the fulfillment of one of the Bible prophecies, which is the birth of Jesus and the embodiment of God's love for mankind.

Nowadays, however, children hear that Easter is all about "colored eggs" and bunnies instead of the power of the resurrected Christ and His plan to save us from our sins—a foundational truth of the Christian faith!

Slanderers are also secular. For instance, for quite some time historians have used the terms "Before Christ-B.C." and "Anno Domini-A.D." as a system to number the years, based on the birth of our Lord Jesus Christ. The phrase "*anno Domini*", in Latin, is translated "*in the year of the Lord*".

However, in recent times the "B.C." has been changed to "Before Common Era-B.C.E." and the "A.D." to "After Common Era-A.C.E.". These changes were introduced to hide the Christian worldview and to make it more appealing to the secular world that rejects and denies Jesus Christ.

Slandering is the work of the spirit of the antichrist. These days even churches encourage the celebration of Halloween and the spirit of death, as long as kids wear angel costumes and have fun. In every instance, these things slander the Christian faith and reject Jesus Christ and the good news of the Gospel. The day is coming to judge all!

Lack of Self Control

God gave us a spirit of self control (also called self-discipline) (2 Timothy 1:7). Those who are saved and have received the gift of God can also lose control of themselves. It is impossible to bring back to repentance those who have tasted the Spirit of God and then fallen away from the faith in Jesus Christ (Hebrews 6:4-6). Those that have not tasted the Spirit of God also lack self control. A lack of self-control in turn leads to hatred, brutality and murder.

The Holy Bible instructs us to crucify the flesh daily and live in the Spirit, to prevent ongoing injury to our soul. The soul becomes weary, discouraged, and pierced as a result of the conflict between the flesh and the Spirit (Hebrews 12:3 & 1 Peter 2:11). James called this "desires that battle within us" (James 4:1). The flesh and the Spirit wage war against each other and the winner always compels the soul to yield to it. It looks like most of the good characters we used to have, have become extinct, and we think we are wiser than when we first got saved. We have forgotten our "first love" and have become "lukewarm" (Revelation 2:4 and 3:16). May God forgive us!

Lovers of Pleasure
Millions of dollars are spent each year on pleasure and entertainment. A great majority of people are in deeper debt than ever before because they are addicted to shopping and spending millions to satisfy the desires of their flesh and in the hope of finding joy and happiness.

"Personal debt increased from $805 billion in 1990 to $1.65 trillion in 2001, and 40% of Americans say they live beyond their means. The personal savings rate as a percentage of GDP (Gross Domestic Product) decreased from 7.5% in the early 80's to 2.4% in 2002. During World War II, Americans were saving more than 24%." (eFinancialPortals, 2010).

The Church
Finally, the Apostle Paul addresses the church, to those who are saved but have drifted away from the faith, in his second letter to Timothy. In Matthew 24:10, Jesus also warned that many Christians would fall away in the

last days, because they love money and their bellies more than they love God. Some pastors have even become "lost shepherds" instead of keeping the flock from the wolf, who is Satan that comes to steal, kill, and destroy.

Division in the Church

In 2008, *Christianity Today* magazine reported the division in the U.S. Episcopal Church as one of the top ten stories of the year 2007 (Top Ten Stories of 2007, 2007). As a result of this division, in 2008, a new "rival church" was created by conservatives of the Anglican Church of North America. This new "rival church" is expected to displace the Episcopal Church, according to *Christianity Today* magazine (Conservative Anglicans Create Rival Church. Top leader Duncan expects to see Episcopal Church 'displaced', 2008).

In November of 2010, *Charisma Magazine* also reported on its website an article entitled "*Is it ok to be gay and Christian?*" It reported the story of one pastor who admitted to his congregation that he was gay. In addition, the article mentioned the related issue of gays serving in the church and how it was causing a division among the members of the two major denominations: the Episcopal Church USA and the Evangelical Lutheran Church in America (Grady, 2010).

As a result, in August of 2010, the members of the Evangelical Lutheran Church in America were divided and those opposing gay clergy formed a new denomination church, the North American Lutheran Church. All these divisions are caused due to the crisis the church is facing today. This is a defeat for the church as a whole. In fact, the Apostle Paul wrote to the Corinthians that they had been defeated because of the divisions in the church (1 Corinthians 6:7). The church has to wake up now, before it is too late.

Church Scandals and Abuse of Children

The church is paying millions and millions because of child abuses and sexual scandals. The following report is from *USA Today* on child sexual abuses by the Catholic Church in the United States: "Dioceses in the United States have paid more than 2.6 billion US dollars in abuse-related costs since 1950's" (Zoll, 2009). In 2005 alone, dioceses in the United States had made financial settlements with the victims totaling over 467 million U.S. dollars (Milligan, 2006). It is now all too common for Christians and church leaders to be caught up in sex scandals and for driving while drunk or under the influence (DUI). Thank God for the true and good shepherd—Jesus Christ. Jesus said, "I am the good shepherd." (John 10:11). Those who call themselves "*shepherds*" but are not called by the Holy Spirit do not own the church or its members! Some of these "*shepherds*" even tried to incorporate churches as "businesses."

The church is the house of God and Jesus will soon return to cleanse "His temple". "There is only one Lawgiver and Judge, the one who is able to save and destroy." (James 4:12). Jesus said, "All authority in heaven and on earth has been given to me." (Matthew 28:18). The authority to judge is given to Jesus and He will be judging all at the appointed time!

The Great Tribulation

The end times will be a time of tribulations and pestilence. The Great Tribulation will include wars and famine (Revelation 6:3-6), as well as earthquakes and signs of the shaking of the heavens. Another sign will be the persecution of the church, which will be covered in the next Chapter. Jesus warned us in advance of the events to come so we can be ready, strengthening ourselves in our most holy faith, becoming absolutely passionate about our first love, Jesus.

Revelation 6 discusses the opening of the fourth seal and all the terrible things that will accompany it. Those who escaped the wars and famine will face death by plague. Revelations 6:7-8 says, "I heard the voice of the fourth living creature saying, "Come and see." So I looked, and behold, a pale horse. And the name of him who sat on it was Death, and Hades followed with him. And power was given to them over a fourth of the earth, to kill with sword, with hunger and plague, with death, and by the beasts of the earth."

Jerusalem and the Desolation of Temple

Jesus foretold the destruction of the Temple, during the tribulation time, by saying, "I tell you the truth, not one stone here will be left on another; everyone will be thrown down." (Matthew 24:2). He also foretold the destruction of Jerusalem. "When you see Jerusalem being surrounded by armies, you will know that its desolation is near" (Luke 21:20).

The antichrist, "the abomination that causes desolation" (Matthew 24:15), will be standing in the temple of God in Jerusalem, the holy place. At that time, those in Israel will flee to the mountains (Matthew 24:16). In those days, there will be great tribulation. Thank God for shortening the time for the sake of the elect (Matthew 24:22).

<u>Signs in the Heavens</u>

Finally, signs will be seen in the heavens and the heavenly bodies will be shaken, just before the appearing of the Lord Jesus Christ. "The sun will be darkened, and the moon will not give its light;" (Mark 13:24). In conclusion, when all these things happen, we need to stand and lift up our heads as our redemption is near (Luke 21:25-28). Jesus is coming! See Part 2 for the tables of the Pre-Tribulation and Tribulations and the Great Tribulation.

CHAPTER 5:

PERSECUTION OF THE CHURCH

*"But before all this, they will lay hands on you and persecute
you. They will deliver you to synagogues and prisons,
and you will be brought before kings and governors,
and all on account of my name."*
(Luke 21:12)

Persecution of the Church

Christians are those who passionately love and serve Jesus Christ, and represent the church. The word "Christian" came from the Greek word *"Christianos (khris-tee-an-os')"* and is translated as *"follower of Christ"*. Today in the Western world the term "Christian" seems to include anyone who thinks he is good enough to get to heaven. However, to be a Christian or a true follower of Jesus, one must have a personal relationship with Jesus Christ by accepting Him as his or her personal Lord and Savior. In the Holy Bible, the word "Christian" only appears three times. See Chapter 9 for what one must do to be saved.

Persecution of those who follow the almighty God is not a new thing. Scriptures give us several examples of persecution for the faith. Old Testament believers of God were persecuted for believing that He was the One and only God, Jehovah. In the New Testament, the meaning of persecution is the suffering of Christians for the sake of Jesus as witnesses to unbelievers (Mark 13:9). This persecution occurs because of Jesus (Mark 13:13) and His name (Luke 21:12).

Many instances of persecution are recorded in the Old Testament Scriptures. Some of these include: the rejection of Jeremiah's prophecy and his sufferings (Jeremiah 15:10-21), Daniel in the lions' den (Daniel 6:1-17), the challenges faced by Nehemiah to build the walls of Jerusalem (Nehemiah 4:1-3), the attempt to wipe out or persecute the Jews in the time of Esther (Esther 3:6), and finally we find the beheading of John the Baptist (Mark 6:17-29) that happened before the cross, and hence is categorized as happened in the Old Testament period. The persecution of

Christians also continued in the New Testament period and it started with the crucifixion of Jesus (Mark 14:61-65).

The Holy Bible also recounts the persecution of Christians starting with the early church in Acts all the way to the end of time in the Book of Revelation. Other examples of persecution in the New Testament period include the stoning and death of Stephen, the persecution of Christians of the early church, and the resulting scattering of Christians to other parts of the world (Acts 7:1-8:3). See Part 2 for the table of the Pre-Tribulation and Tribulations.

In addition, most of the early disciples of Jesus actually died because of persecution. A study of church history and the Holy Bible reveal the persecutions of followers of Jesus including James (Acts 12:2), Philip, Matthew, Matthias, Andrew, Mark, Peter (Acts 12:3), Paul (Acts 14:19), Jude, Bartholomew, Thomas, Luke, and Barnabas. Since that time, persecution has increased dramatically and continues today. It will not cease until the day Jesus returns. We read in Revelation 6:9-11 that God told those who had died because of their testimonies to wait a little longer, because God is going to avenge their deaths. While God is patient, Jesus will return as the judge at the appointed time.

It is estimated that around 200 million Christians suffer persecution worldwide and this number is increasing, according to OpenDoorsUSA.org (Compelling Facts List). OpenDoorsUSA.org is organized to help persecuted Christians around the world. Let's look at the following statistics regarding the persecution of Christians around the world, according to OpenDoorsUSA.org:

"Compelling Facts List

- The world's worst persecutor of Christians in the world is North Korea.
- In Saudi Arabia, practicing Christianity can result in death by beheading or stoning.
- Over 90% of China's Christians worship in hidden, underground house churches to avoid government regulations and restrictions.
- There is only one Christian church left in the Gaza Strip, and its membership has dwindled to less than 100.
- Algeria is about a quarter of the size of Texas, and only 3% of the population is Christians.
- There are 69 languages in Iran, and only three of them have a completed Bible. Iran is also the third worst persecutor of Christians in the world.
- It is believed there are less than 500 Christians living in the Maldives.
- Open preaching in Sudan is punishable by beatings or imprisonment.
- Christians make up less than 1.7% of the population in Pakistan, and over 70% of them are the poorest of the poor.
- It is estimated that there are 1,100 Christian missionaries living in Turkey." (Compelling Facts List).

Following is a list of the top fifty countries that are persecuting Christians with their ranking:

The World Watch List	
RANK	COUNTRY
1	KOREA. NORTH
2	IRAN
3	SAUDI ARABIA
4	SOMALIA
5	MALDIVES
6	AFGHANISTAN
7	YEMEN
8	MAURITANIA
9	LAOS
10	UZBEKISTAN
11	ERITREA
12	BHUTAN
13	CHINA
14	PAKISTAN
15	TURKMENISTAN
16	COMOROS
17	IRAQ
18	QATAR
19	CHECHNYA
20	EGYPT
21	VIETNAM
22	LIBYA
23	BURMA/MYANMAR
24	AZERBAIJAN
25	ALGERIA
26	INDIA
27	NIGERI
28	OMAN
29	BRUNEI
30	SUDAN
31	KUWAIT
32	TAJIKISTAN
33	UNITED ARAB EMIRATES
34	ZANZIBAR ISLANDS-(TANZANIA)
35	TURKEY
36	DJIBOUTI
37	MOROCCO
38	CUBA
39	JORDAN
40	SRI LANKA
41	SYRIA
42	BELARUS
43	TUNISIA
44	ETHIOPIA
45	BANGLADESH
46	PALESTINIAN TERRITORY
47	BAHRAIN
48	INDONESIA
49	KYRGYZSTAN
50	KENYA NORTH EAST

(World Watch List, 2010)

In conclusion, Christians must accept both the blessings of God and the pain that Jesus bore on the cross, because it is a privilege to suffer for Jesus' sake (Philippians 1:29). Jesus called "blessed" those who will be persecuted because of righteousness (Luke 6:22). The men and women of faith are also commended for their faith and sufferings in Hebrews 11:35-40, where it says they became witnesses for Jesus and faced various persecutions to gain a better resurrection, and the world was not worthy of them. Those persecuted for Jesus have their reward in heaven. The reward of the persecuted Christians is a hundred fold and eternal life (Mark 10:30). Christians also need to voice their concerns over and pray for the persecuted church. Hold onto your faith until the end, because Jesus is coming soon!

CHAPTER 6:
WORLDWIDEEVANGELISM

"Go into all the world and preach the good news
to all creation."
(Mark 16:15)

World Wide Evangelism

The Gospel is one and only one and unchangeable (Galatians 1:6-8). We must not change the message in any way, for it is the good news of salvation to a lost and dying world, and it doesn't need our help to make it more palatable. The message of the Gospel (the Good News) is that God gave His only begotten and beloved Son to save the world. Its message is sacred and gives eternal life to all who believe. The Gospel is unfailing, just as the love of God and His mercy and favor (grace) never fail (1 Corinthians 13:8).

The Gospel is also a message of reconciliation of men with God. When we believe there is only one God (Deuteronomy 6:4) and that His Son Jesus came from God (John 17:3) to die on the cross, and pay the penalty for our sins, we receive eternal life. When we believe, we receive the everlasting love and the eternal covenant of God, the New Testament (Jeremiah 31:3). The Gospel is able to save all who believe in it. It was able to save people 2,000 years ago; it still saves today; and it will continue to save till Jesus comes back.

The Holy Bible instructs us to go into the entire world from east to west to preach the Good News or the Gospel of peace through Jesus Christ (Acts 10:36). The preaching of the Gospel started when John the Baptist paved the way for Jesus, and then Jesus preached and passed it onto His disciples.

The disciples then preached the Gospel everywhere from Jerusalem to Judea and Samaria. When the Jews rejected the Gospel and the persecution of the Christians of the Jerusalem church started, the disciples went to preach to the Gentiles. The spread of the Gospel is so vital and urgent that Jesus commissioned the disciples to take it into the entire world. This idea did not originate with the disciples, but in the heart of God, who yearned for all mankind to be saved.

Sharing the Gospel is not merely the job of pastors and full time ministers, but is the duty of all who are born again. If we are disciples of Jesus, we need to preach the Gospel to everyone as a testimony to all nations (Mark 13:10) and before the end comes (Matthew 24:14). We must be assertive and bold to fulfill such a tremendous responsibility and calling! Jesus commissioned the disciples to witness the Gospel to the unsaved. The word commission means "to order, to command, to appoint, to charge, and to anoint".

A good parallel to the commissioning of the disciples by Jesus is found in the Old Testament in Numbers 27:19 when God told Moses to commission Joshua. Joshua was commissioned with the responsibility of leading the Israelites to the Promised Land. Christians are disciples who are expected to witness Jesus to the unsaved so that whoever believes in Jesus and confesses that Jesus is Lord will be saved and be part of the kingdom of God.

In the Old Testament, Moses interceded with God so that the Israelites were forgiven of their sins (Exodus 33:12-17). David prayed asking permission to build a house for God (2 Samuel 7:2). Daniel prayed, fasted, and repented for his people's return from Babylon to Jerusalem (Daniel 9:1-21). Esther and her people fasted and prayed so that she would find favor with the king to ask for the lives of her people to be spared (Esther 4:16). Nehemiah prayed and fasted for the construction of the walls of Jerusalem (Nehemiah 1:4-11). Jesus also prayed and fasted for forty days before beginning His ministry on earth. In addition, the Apostle Paul was broken hearted and in great sorrow for the sake of the people of Israel, even to the point of being accursed and cut off from Christ (Romans 9:1-3). We therefore need to fast, pray, and intercede for the unsaved. We must to burn with passion for the house of God and be consumed by the Holy Fire for the salvation of the unsaved.

In addition, witnessing to the unsaved is not granted to the angels but to Christians or believers (Acts 10:5). We need to watch and be content with our living styles and allocate the first fruit of our time, daily to the witnessing of the Gospel to the unsaved.

Every believer of Jesus should be a witness of Jesus by testifying to the resurrection of Jesus and sharing the word of God with those who need it most. Jesus is also faithful to keep His promises to go with those who evangelize and to manifest with signs and wonders (Mark 16:20). When the Gospel is preached as Philip did in Samaria (Acts 8:5), signs and wonders will follow.

Ways of Evangelism

The Gospel is preached in almost all the seven continents of the world in different ways including:

- Street preaching or one to one evangelism
- Teachings or sermons
- Revival meetings or conferences
- Assisting or supporting churches and ministries in evangelism (contribution and support by church members in various ways including financial contributions, prayers, and volunteering)
- Translation and distribution of the Holy Bible, religious books, and booklets on various doctrines

- Monthly Christian magazines
- Radio or TV broadcasts (televangelism), and
- Internet

Worldwide Translation of the Holy Bible

One way of disseminating the Gospel throughout the world is by means of translation and distribution of the Holy Bible. The United Bible Societies (UBS) is made up of 145 national Bible societies that work together to translate the Holy Bible into many different languages of the world, and distribute them all over the world. These Bible societies are from over 200 countries and territories (About UBS, 2008).

The Holy Bible is translated into many languages of the world. See the tables below for details of translations and distributions of the Holy Bible by the major UBS areas, as of December 31, 2009 (Scripture Translation, 2009).

Area	Total number of translations
Africa	731
Asia-Pacific	1,052
Europe-Middle East	210
Americas	512
Constructed Languages	3
Total	2,508

2009 Worldwide Distribution of the Holy Bible, retrieved November 1, 2010 (Scripture Distribution 2009, 2009):

UBS AREA	Bibles	Testaments	Portions	New Reader Portions	Selections	New Reader Selections
AFRICA	5,144,755	436,268	810,371	46,514	4,535,208	87,212
AMERICAS	12,133,950	2,797,084	5,345,443	3,060,941	258,921,645	53,460,095
ASIA - PACIFIC	9,976,994	6,978,178	7,208,093	3,912,460	46,831,034	3,635,879
EUROPE MIDDLE EAST	2,135,577	982,082	1,716,376	320,661	582,483	83,918
TOTAL DISTRIBUTION	29,391,276	11,193,612	15,080,283	7,340,576	310,870,370	57,267,122

According to Howard Culbertson, Southern Nazarene University, distribution of the Holy Bible per year, as of 2008, is as follows:

Scripture distribution (all sources)	
Bibles per year	53,700,000
New Testaments per year	120,700,000
Scripture portions per year	4,600 million

(Statistics: The 21st century world, 2008)

Challenges of World Wide Evangelism

There is, however, a great need to evangelize more than ever to those who live in countries located in the "10/40 window". Of the 55 least evangelized countries, 97% of their population live within the "10/40 window", according to statistics gathered by Howard

64

Culbertson, Southern Nazarene University (10/40 Window: Do you need to be stirred to action?, 2010).

The "10/40 Window" is the rectangular area that covers North Africa, the Middle East, and Asia between 10 degrees and 40 degrees north latitude from the equator. This area is populated by the majority of the world's Muslims, Hindus, Buddhists, and those who have no religious beliefs. Today Christian ministries and churches face the following challenges:

- Continuing the task of witnessing and making disciples
- Lack of focus and resources on the planting of new churches
- Spiritual challenges (the persecution of Christians)
- Local religious and cultural barriers (fundamentalism and a resistance to the Gospel)
- Political or national barriers (certain countries may not be open to Christianity)
- Language barriers (need for translation of the Bible into different languages and to train evangelists the different languages of the world), and
- Location obstacles (a vast majority of the unreached live in remote and inaccessible areas).

Christians and the church, therefore, should focus on the mission of preaching the Gospel, i.e., "Preaching Jesus". The church should not be like a market place of different ideas modeled after the secular world. The church is the house of God and belongs to Jesus because He paid the price through His innocent and holy and righteous blood (Acts 20:28).

God will not tolerate those who use the church for their own advantage and entertain their own ideas rather than preaching the message of the cross. See Part 2 for the table of the Pre-Tribulation and Tribulations. In conclusion, we have to do the work of the Lord while "it is day" (John 9:4). Jesus gave us a mission to complete before He returns (Luke 19:13). We must witness for Christ so that Jesus is not ashamed of us when He returns (Luke 9:26). We must be faithful in serving the Lord to finally receive the crown of glory (1 Peter 5:4).

PART 3:
GET READY

"Therefore keep watch, because you do not know on what day your Lord will come"
(Matthew 24:42)

CHAPTER 7:
HOW TO GET READY FOR THE LAST HOUR?

"Since everything will be destroyed in this way, what kind of people ought you to be? You ought to live holy and godly lives"
(2 Peter 3:11)

How to Get Ready For the Last Hour?

So how do we wait for and get ready for the day of the Lord? The Holy Bible tells us to get ready, when the end is near, and wait for "the blessed hope—the glorious appearing of our great God and Savior, Jesus Christ" (Titus 2:13). To be part of the kingdom of God, one must first be born again by believing in Jesus, the Son of God. See Chapter 9 to learn more about how to be saved. Once saved and have a personal relationship with God, we must prepare our hearts including the following:

Holiness

The word "holiness", in Hebrew, is "*qodesh*" and it means "*consecrated, sacred, or set apart*". The Apostle Peter explains it by saying, "make every effort to be found spotless, blameless, and at peace with him" (2 Peter 3:14) so that we can inherit eternal life and the home of righteousness, a new heaven and a new earth. Holiness, living blamelessly before God, will be more important than ever as the days grow more lawless and sin flourishes as never before. As the darkness grows ever darker, the light of holiness and truth will be clearly visible to those with eyes to see. Time is running out!

The Apostle Peter also warns that the heavens and earth will be destroyed by fire and therefore we need to live holy and godly (2 Peter 3:10-14). Holiness is the character of Jesus that must also characterize us, as we clothe ourselves in it, to deny the desires of our flesh. (Romans 13:14). We need to be holy to see God, to understand His plan for us, and finally to be able to hear what God says to us (Hebrews 12:14).

Self-control

Men will be lacking self control in the end times. The Apostle Peter warns, "the end of all things is near" and goes on to say, be "clear minded and self controlled so that you can pray" (1 Peter 4:7). The Apostle Paul also wrote "let us be self-controlled" so that believers are not shaken and without faith in the end times (1 Thessalonians 5:8).

It is important that we have a clear vision about the end times and what God's plan is for us, so that we know how to live the Christian life, walk the Christian walk, and as David said, "to number our days aright, that we may gain a heart of wisdom" (Psalm 90:12). We can understand the times only when we can think clearly and avoid confusion. God gave us a spirit of self-control and we need to exercise it so that we stay focused on what is coming, the day of the Lord! Self-control is a fruit of the Holy Spirit together with love, joy, peace, and patience (Galatians 5:22). And though the patience of the saints will be tested during the last days, we must be patient until the Lord returns (James 5:7-9).

Love

Love is the most important thing we need to have in the end times, as men will be lovers of money and themselves. Jesus foretold that in the last days the love of many would grow cold (Matthew 24:12). Love is what we received from God through Jesus and we have to give it back to others, especially when the end is near. The three spiritual qualities Christians should have are faith, hope, and love and the greatest of these is love (1 Corinthians 13:13). Note that only love remains in the end because faith and hope will be fulfilled with the second coming of Jesus Christ. Let's let the love of God flow through us to reach a lost and dying world!

The Apostle Peter instructs us to "love each other deeply" (1 Peter 4:8) and to "offer hospitality to one another without grumbling" (1 Peter 4:9). We need to continue to love each other and welcome each other. In addition, when the end is near, we need "to serve others, faithfully administrating God's grace in its various forms" (1 Peter 4:10) and not to judge others till Jesus comes back again (1 Corinthians 4:5).

Encouragement and Fellowship

Encouragement will be vitally important in the last days because most people will lose hope, be confused, and struggle to hold onto faith. The Apostle Paul stressed the need to encourage each other with the word of God in his letter to the Thessalonians: "Therefore encourage each other with these words" (1 Thessalonians 4:18). We must be encouraged with the hope of the second coming of Jesus, the resurrection of believers, the hope of having eternal life, and living with Christ forever. As we love and encourage each other, our faith will grow so we can hold onto the hope within us. Encouragement comes from love and it builds Christians. It also strengthens our faith in Jesus. "Encourage one another and build each other up" (1 Thessalonians 5:11).

The Apostle Paul also stressed the importance of encouragement by finally saying the following blessing on the Thessalonians, "May our Lord Jesus Christ himself and God our Father, who loved us and by his grace gave us eternal encouragement and good hope, encourage your hearts and strengthen you in every good deed and word." (2 Thessalonians 2:16-17). In addition, the writer of Hebrews encourages Christians to continue to have fellowship and encourage one another, when the end is near, by saying, "Let us not give up meeting together, as some are in the habit of doing, but let us encourage one another" (Hebrews 10:25).

Faith and Perseverance

Faith is what God expects from every believer. It is the evidence of things not seen, a gift of the Holy Spirit, and without faith it will be impossible to persevere through the difficult days ahead. Faith comes by hearing the true word of God (Ephesians 1:13 and Romans 10:17). The Apostle Paul wrote to the Thessalonians to hold onto their faith in Jesus Christ (2 Thessalonians 2:15). Faith is central to Christianity in that we are saved by faith and faith pleases God.

Anything we do apart from faith is sin, according to Scriptures. Faith makes our hope real and certain of what we have not yet seen (Hebrews 11:1). Our faith is tested in the end times and therefore we need to endure and persevere with the help and grace of God given to us through Jesus Christ. So in the end times, we need faith to look forward and to wait with patience for the day of the Lord (2 Peter 3:12). By faith we can also look forward to see the promises of God, including a new heaven and a new earth, which is the home of the righteous! (2 Peter 3:13). If we are saved by accepting Jesus as our savior, then we should not be troubled by the second coming of the Lord, as we are in the light and not in darkness anymore (John 14:1-3).

Watch and Pray

The phrase "to watch", in Greek, is "*blepó*" and it is defined as "*to beware, to be careful, to be on guard, to keep on seeing, sight, and taking care"* while the phrase "to pray", in Hebrew, is *"palal"*, which means *"to intercede, make supplication, and to mediate"*. Prayer is an act of faith. Praying involves faith to see things first in the spirit realm before they are manifested in the natural realm. We should pray only if we have the faith and hope that God will listen and answer our prayers. If we do not believe our prayers will be answered, we pray in vain. Prayer actually has the power to strengthen us and give us encouragement when we need it the most.

Being watchful and prayerful also keeps us from falling into temptations. That is why we should pray every day, "Our father in heaven…And lead us not into temptation, but deliver us from the evil one" (Matthew 6:9-13). We need to pray and love to seek the face of God daily. We need to pray continually (1 Thessalonians 5:17). Our prayers are more effective when we know and understand the times in which we live.

In addition, we will be delivered and escape the snares of the devil, when we watch and pray. Prayer helps us escape from things that happen in this world that are not from God and it will keep us from the coming wrath of God. Prayer and being watchful make us ready for the day of the Lord (Matthew 24:42-50). We need to be alert and pray because we do not know the day or the hour of Jesus' return (Mark 13:33). In conclusion, we need to be eagerly awaiting the soon return of our wonderful Lord Jesus (1 Thessalonians 1:10).

CHAPTER 8:

THE CHURCH AND JESUS' PROMISES

"And he made known to us the mystery of his will according to his good pleasure, which he purposed in Christ, to be put into effect when the times will have reached their fulfillment—to bring all things in heaven and on earth together under one head, even Christ"
(Ephesians 1:9-10)

The Church and Jesus' Promises

The church, also known as the body of Christ, is represented by Christians- those who are passionately in love with the Lord Jesus Christ. In the last trying days ahead, it will be essential for believers to hold tightly to the promises of God, in order to be patient, not to lose hope of His coming, and finally to be rescued from the coming wrath of God. God's plan for the church is to bring together all things in heaven and earth under Jesus (Ephesians 1:10) whose promises for the church relating to the end times include the following:

Satan, the Antichrist, and the False Prophets will be Destroyed

After all the signs of Jesus' coming are fulfilled, He will be revealed and glorified (2 Thessalonians 1:10 & Colossians 3:4). When Jesus comes in all His splendor, He will first throw the antichrist and the false prophet into the lake of fire (Revelation 19:20 & 2 Thessalonians 2:8). Satan will then be captured and chained for 1,000 years and Jesus will establish the millennium kingdom. After the millennium kingdom rule, Jesus will destroy and throw Satan into the lake of fire, where he will burn forever (Revelation 20:10).

Christians will be Saved from the Coming Wrath of God

The days of tribulation will be shortened for the sake of the elect (believers) in Christ (Mark 13:20). Jesus is the one who can rescue and save us from the coming wrath of God (1 Thessalonians 1:10)! God will, however, punish those who do not know Him and those who refuse to obey the Gospel of Jesus Christ (2 Thessalonians 1:7-9). When Jesus comes, He will establish the millennium kingdom (Revelation 20:6). In the end times, for Christians it will be a time of rejoicing rather than a time of sorrow, because "the sun of righteousness will rise" (Malachi 4:2). Jesus promised to return to take us so that we may be with Him forever (John 14:1-3). Jesus is the way to the Father.

A New Heaven and a New Earth

We as believers have the promise of God that He is preparing a place for us, so we should be excited and anticipate it with great joy. Scriptures call it the "new heaven and earth" (2 Peter 3:13). If we know Jesus as our personal Savior, it won't be long before we see the new heaven and the new earth as the time is at hand! "But you have come to Mount Zion, to the heavenly Jerusalem, the city of the living God. You have come to thousands upon thousands of angels in joyful assembly, to the church of the firstborn, whose names are written in heaven. You have come to God, the judge of all men, to the spirits of righteous men made perfect, to Jesus the mediator of a new covenant, and to the sprinkled blood that speaks a better word than the blood of Abel" (Hebrews 12:22-24). By faith, we are already in the kingdom of God! This is the faith we have in Jesus.

Peace and Justice

Jesus gave us complete and abundant peace through His blood (John 14:27), when we accepted Him as our Savior and were justified by faith. This peace is ours because we have access to the grace of God and His presence (Romans 5:1). The peace is a gift of God, which is the assurance that we have eternal life in Jesus. His perfect peace also brings His people both favor and healing.

God is just and Jesus will bring not only real peace but also justice to the nations of the earth (Isaiah 42:3-4). God will restore everything as He just promised (Acts 3:19-21). When Jesus, the Root of Jesse comes, He will deliver the whole creation order (Isaiah 11:6-9), and creation itself will be liberated from the bondage of decay (Romans 8:19-22).

Resurrection and Eternal Life

Scriptures say that when Jesus comes, the dead in Christ will rise again first. They will not face the second death (the eternal death), which is the lake of fire, but will have everlasting life (Revelation 20:14). Jesus destroyed the power of death and took the keys of Hades from the devil, when He rose from the dead (Revelation 1:18). We have the hope of resurrection that is promised to us by Jesus. This hope is the result of the death and the resurrection of Jesus Christ from the dead. It is a living hope and helps us not to be troubled and to have faith and trust in God. Jesus Christ has given us the promise of eternal life (1 John 2:25) and God's kingdom is an eternal kingdom (Psalms 145:13). Jesus is the giver of the water of life (John 4:10) and the everlasting life (John 3:36). Finally, the inheritance of this hope is kept in heaven. It cannot perish, spoil, or fade away, but is shielded and protected by the power of God until the end times (1 Peter 1:3-6). This inheritance is allotted to Christians and Christians shall receive it!

Discernment

Discerning the spirit of the antichrists, through the gifts of the Holy Spirit, is given to the church (believers) (1 Corinthians 12:10; 1 John 2:20, 27; and John 16:7-13).

Through the gift of discerning the spirits, we can discern antichrists and false prophets of our times. The Holy Spirit leads us to the truth and helps us to know the truth, and that truth is Jesus Christ. Because of receiving the Holy Spirit we are not orphans, left alone in this world. In conclusion, Jesus promised the Holy Spirit (John 14:16-18) so that we can know the future and discern the end times. Jesus also gave the church the authority over wicked spirits to discern and resist them (Ephesians 6:10-17). God bless you for reading this far. Finally, please read the following Chapter entitled "Salvation—What must you do to be saved?" to learn more about how to be saved, and also use it as a witnessing tool to win others.

CHAPTER 9:
SALVATION — WHAT MUST YOU DO TO BE SAVED?

"Then they asked him, "What must we do to do the works God
requires?" Jesus answered, "The work of God is this:
to believe in the one he has sent. "
(John 6:28-29)

What is Salvation, and how can You Escape the Coming Wrath of God?

The word "salvation", in Hebrew, is *"yeshuah"* and is defined as *"deliverance and help, security and victory"* or simply to *"save"*. It is mentioned for the first time in the Old Testament, according to the Easton's Bible Dictionary, to signify *"the deliverance the LORD will bring"* to the Israelites from the bondage of slavery by the Egyptians (Exodus 14:13). In addition, it signifies the deliverance from evil or danger in general (Easton's Bible Dictionary). In the New Testament however, the meaning has additional emphasis and it signifies the greatness of our salvation. It is called the great deliverance from sin or *"a great salvation"* (Hebrews 2:3).

This new salvation was first announced by the Lord Jesus Christ. The word "salvation", in Greek, is *"sótéria"* and has additional meaning beyond "deliverance". It does include *"preservation, to rescue or safety, and health"*. Salvation is being delivered or deliverance from eternal death to eternal life. Jesus Himself is eternal life. And not only do we inherit eternal life; we are indeed healed by His stripes and received eternal peace and rest!

According to Noah Webster's New International Dictionary of the English Language, "salvation" is defined as, *"the act of saving; preservation or deliverance from destruction, danger, or great calamity. Salvation is the redemption of man from the bondage of sin and liability to eternal death, and the conferring on him of everlasting happiness"* (Easton's Bible Dictionary).

Sin, Judgment, and Death - "WHY we Need to be Saved"

"The LORD God formed the man from the dust of the ground and breathed into his nostrils the breath of life, and the man became a living being" (Genesis 2:7). God created man for eternity, to rule the earth, and have dominion. The first sin was committed in the Garden of Eden, when Adam and Eve fell from the grace of God. Adam and Eve believed the lie of Satan (the old serpent) and ate of the fruit God forbid them to eat (Genesis 2:16-17 & Genesis 3:6).

Because of Adam's disobedience to God, death was introduced to this world through one man. Since the time of Adam and Eve, death reigned on all men as a result of the sin committed by one man (Romans 5:12). Sin is rebellion or disobedience against God and His commandments, and results in eternal separation from God. Sin also separates man from relationship with God. Therefore, obedience is very important for our spiritual walk and growth. The cost of sin is so great that God gave His Son to be crucified and pay the penalty for our sins and redeem us back to Him. "He was pierced for our transgressions," (Isaiah 53:5).

Death is the wages of sin and as a result, Adam was sentenced to die for what he did (Genesis 3:19). In the Old Testament, King Solomon noted that the flesh or the dust returns to the ground it came from, while the spirit of man returns to God who gave it (Ecclesiastes 12:7). In the New Testament, the writer of Hebrews also noted that because of sin "man is destined to die once, and after that to face judgment" (Hebrews 9:27). We, therefore, need to be saved from eternal death and separation from God because we are all sinners and have fallen from the grace of God (Romans 3:23).

God's Love - "WHERE our Saving Grace all Started or Came From"

The Apostle Paul reminds us that "the grace of God that brings salvation has appeared to all men" (Titus 2:11). God did not leave us as orphans and let us die in our sins, but He designed a way to save us even from the foundation of the world through Jesus Christ (Ephesians 1:4). While salvation is free for anyone who wants to receive it, it cost God His precious Son, Jesus Christ (Ephesians 1:6).

God has a purpose for our lives. God's heart for all humanity is that all be saved and escape eternal death (1st Timothy 2:3-6). He does not want all or anyone to perish. God did not send Jesus to condemn the world but to forgive (John 3:17). The decision to accept Jesus as our savior is left to us. God does not compel us to accept Him as He gave us the free will to choose our destiny. We must, however, choose life to live (Deuteronomy 30:19)!

God is not a respecter of persons, but calls all to repentance to come to the knowledge of His Son Jesus Christ (2 Peter 3:9). If we believe in Jesus and that He is the Son of God, God promised us eternal life (John 3:16). We have been offered this gift of salvation so that we inherit eternal life (Romans 6:23).

Thank God for sending us Jesus so that the grace we all lost through Adam can be restored to us through believing in Jesus (Romans 5:15-16). In fact, we have received the fullness and riches of His grace through receiving Jesus (John 1:16). In this, we see how deep the love of God is for us. The Apostle Paul asked, "Who shall separate us from the love of Christ?" (Romans 8:35). No one indeed!

The Cross, the Atoning Sacrifice, and the Resurrection - "HOW we are Saved"

1. The Cross

A cross or a tree was used in Old Testament times to crucify a sinful man worthy of death. The cross signifies a curse. The sinful man crucified was also considered under God's curse. The body of a crucified man was not to be left on the cross overnight and had to be buried the same day, so as not to desecrate the land as was the custom of the Jews (Deuteronomy 21:22-23).

Likewise, Jesus was crucified and was buried on the same day to save all who would choose to believe in Him. The cross is like the altar of God in the New Testament and Jesus was the atoning sacrifice. The cross also signifies the reconciliation of God with man. God reconciled us to Himself through the crucifixion of Jesus (2 Corinthians 5:18).

2. The Atoning Sacrifice

Atonement is *"being at one or being reconciled to God"*. Atonement is also defined as *"being merciful, to cover over, to cancel, to forgive, to pardon, to purge away, and to cleanse sins"*. Atonement by sacrificing a lamb was common for forgiveness of sins in the Old Testament time, for life is in the blood and it is the blood that makes atonement for one's life (Leviticus 17:11). In the New Testament also, we see that there is no remission or forgiveness of sins without the shedding of blood (Hebrews 9:22).

The practice of atonement by sacrificing a lamb in the Old Testament was a foreshadowing of what was to happen to Jesus and was fulfilled when He was crucified and became the atonement sacrifice for our sins. Jesus fulfilled all the requirements of the law, which the first Adam could not do (1 Peter 1:19). The penalty for our sins was paid on the cross when Jesus was crucified, redeeming us from the curse of the law (Galatians 3:13).

The redemption and forgiveness of our sins was made possible through the blood of Jesus, when He died on the cross and became an atoning sacrifice for us (Ephesians 1:7 and 1 John 2:2). Because Jesus did not sin, His blood was without blemish or defect, making Him the perfect sacrifice to atone for our sins.

3. The Resurrection

Jesus was crucified, died, and buried according to the Scriptures. However, He did not remain dead but rather was raised from the dead on the third day, thus conquering death! Death came to all men because of Adam, but Jesus, the second Adam, gave us back the life we lost when He was resurrected on the third day (1 Corinthians 15:21-22).

By being resurrected, Jesus overcame death! Jesus said in Revelation 1:18 "I am the Living One; I was dead, and behold I am alive forever and ever! And I hold the keys of death and Hades". See Part 2 for the tables of the 1st Resurrection and 2nd Resurrection.

Faith and Grace – "By WHAT we are Saved"

We are saved by the grace of God through faith in Jesus Christ (Ephesians 2:8). Salvation or grace is a favor of God while grace or mercy is an unmerited or free gift from God (Romans 5:16). Jesus is the gift of God who gives eternal life. You can only be saved by the grace of God and not by works.

All must be born again to be saved. Being born again means you become a new creation in Christ (2 Corinthians 5:17).

Steps to Receive Jesus Christ

Step 1-Admitting Sin

We are all sinners and need Jesus. You must admit that you are a sinner and must make a choice or decision to be saved. You cannot do anything on your own to be saved or to be spiritually fruitful (John 15:5). Jesus said, "You have no life in you" (John 6:53).

You only have the opportunity to choose salvation while you are alive; after death, you forfeit your chance to decide, making hell your permanent dwelling place by default. King Solomon reminds us of the importance of making this decision before it is too late by saying, "Remember your Creator in the days of your youth, before the days of trouble come" (Ecclesiastes 12:1).

Step 2-Repentance

Once you make a choice to accept Jesus as your Savior, you must confess that you have sinned and turn away from your sins (Acts 3:19). Acknowledge your guilt of sin and make a sincere heart decision to turn to God. You also need to turn from the world and anything that would keep you from God. This is called repentance. Salvation and new life comes through the repentance of sins and faith in Jesus Christ (Acts 11:18). Our sins are forgiven because Jesus paid the penalty on the cross for our sins.

Step 3-Beliving in Jesus

Once you repent, you must believe with all of your heart that Jesus is the Son of God and that He lived on earth, died on the cross, was raised from the dead, is now with the Father, and will be returning. This is called the true Gospel. When you hear the true Gospel and accept it with true repentance, you are saved and your name is recorded in heaven in the Lamb's Book of Life. This is the only requirement necessary for salvation. "There is no other name under heaven given to men by which we must be saved" (Acts 4:12). Jesus is the truth, the way to God, and the life (John 14:6). Everyone who believes in Jesus Christ receives the forgiveness of sins through His name (Acts 10:43). Finally, pray in Jesus name and invite Him to come in and live in your heart and control your life through the Holy Spirit. Receive Him as your Lord and Savior.

Spiritual Positions

When you accept Jesus as your Savior, you become a child of God (John 1:12) and you will be sealed with the Holy Spirit (Ephesians 1:13). Believers of Jesus are delivered from the dominion or control of Satan, darkness, death, disobedience, and rebellion to the kingdom of God, accompanied by sovereignty and royal power (Colossians 1:13). Finally, know your identity and spiritual positions in Jesus Christ. See the following table for a comparison of the spiritual positions of a believer in Jesus Christ versus that of a non-believer:

Comparison of Spiritual Positions

Believer of Jesus	Bible Verse	Non-believer of Jesus	Bible Verse
A new creation; Born again	2 Corinthians 5:17; John 3:3, 1 Peter 1:3, 1:23	Old self; Dying in sin/Denied the Kingdom of God	Ephesians 4:22; John 3:5
God's child; Member of Christ's body	Ephesians 1:4-5 Galatians 3:26 Romans 8:14; Ephesians 2:19	Child of disobedience/ wrath; Follows the prince of the power of the air	Ephesians 2:2-3
Accepted and stands firm in the Grace of God	Galatians 2:21, Ephesians 2:4-5; 1 Peter 5:12	May or may not follow the Law; Fallen from Grace	Galatians 3:1-3, 3:10, 4:21; Hebrews 12:15
Built on the foundation of the apostles and prophets, with Christ Jesus as the chief cornerstone; Believes in the true Gospel	Ephesians 2:20-22; Galatians 1:11	Without hope and without God in the world; Follows another (false) gospel	Ephesians 2:12; Galatians 1:6
Saved and justified by Faith in Christ	Galatians 2:15, 3:26 Romans 5:1	Believes to be saved by works (deeds) or by observing the Law	Galatians 2:16
Saved and lives spiritually in Christ/Fruitful of the Spirit;	Ephesians 2:8 Galatians 3:26, 5:22-25;	Lives in the flesh/Does the deeds of the flesh;	Galatians 5:19-21;
Blessed by the new/eternal life;	Galatians 3:13-14; Ephesians 1:7;	Cursed to death;	Galatians 3:10;
Forgiven/Redeemed	1 John 1:9, 2:12; Colossians 1:14, 2:13 Romans 8:1, 1 Peter 1:18	Not forgiven/Sold to sin as a slave	Romans 7:14
Righteous and light of the world	Romans 1:17; 3:21-25; 4:1-6; 5:17	A sinner and is in darkness	John 9:41
Symbolized by the New Testament and Sarah	Galatians 4:26-31	Symbolized by the Old Testament and Hagar	Galatians 4:21-25
Set free, victorious, seated with Christ; No more dominion or influence by Satan	Galatians 5:1, 5:13 Ephesians 2:6; Hebrews 2:14, 15 1 John 3:8	Burdened again by a yoke of slavery (defeat); Influenced and in bondage by sin and Satan	Galatians 5:1; Ephesians 2:2-3
Glorifies the cross	Galatians 6:14-15	Glorifies self	Galatians 6:11-13

89

PART 4:
JESUS IS COMING!

"A day of the LORD is coming"
(Zechariah 14:1)

CHAPTER 9:
CONCLUSION—JESUS IS COMING!

"Surely the day is coming; it will burn like a furnace. All the arrogant and every evildoer will be stubble, and that day that is coming will set them on fire,"
(Malachi 4:1)

This is the Last Hour and Jesus is Coming for Real!

As we have seen in previous Chapters, the signs of the end times are everywhere and it is clear the time is near. Jesus said, "Even so, when you see these things happening, you know that it is near, right at the door" (Mark 13:29). Jesus stressed the urgency of His revelation regarding the end times through His angel by saying "The time is near" (Revelation 1:3). Yes, Jesus will come with His splendor in clouds with power and glory (Mark 13:26), in blazing fire and with His angels (2 Thessalonians 1:7), and with the saints (1 Thessalonians 3:13).

Jesus will come to judge the world in righteousness and His people or believers in His truth. He will rescue or save us from the coming wrath of God. You should not be afraid of the day of the Lord as long as you are in the light. Jesus will return for those who are saved, while He will return to judge the unsaved, the devil, the antichrist, and the false prophets or false Christs.

If you have not accepted Jesus Christ as your Savior, please read about salvation in Chapter 9 and give your life to Jesus. Begin to attend a Bible-teaching church near you and get into fellowship in the Lord. If you are already saved, draw near to God and go deep into His word, asking Him to reveal Himself to you and keep the hope of salvation you have received till the end. Since your redemption is near, look forward to stand up and lift your head up. Jesus' words never pass away!

Do not be Deceived!

According to Scriptures, the devil and the antichrist will try to deceive even the elect in Christ. Do not be deceived by the devil, the antichrists and their spirits, and the false prophets that are in the world. Discern the end times and know the antichrists and false prophets of your time.

Do not also be deceived about the soon return or second coming of Jesus Christ. When Jesus comes, He will not be just seen by a few people but all will see Him, as lightning that comes from the east is visible even in the west! Study the word of God, as the truth is in the word of God and the truth will set you free!

Voice Your Concerns Over and Pray for the Persecuted Church!

Many who know and love Christ are currently facing persecution and even death around the world. As a Christian, you must voice your concerns over and be an advocate for the persecuted church. You also need to pray for the persecuted church and to support those ministries that are serving the persecuted churches, financially and through volunteering, to strengthen and equip them. God will never forget the work you do and the love you show to His people. You will get your reward at the appointed time!

Witness Jesus to Others "as long as it is day"!

Christians must evangelize and do the work of the Lord faithfully while "it is day" or before the night comes, because there will come a time when no one can work. Jesus commissioned and assigned all believers to witness to others about Jesus. Christians need to witness for Jesus, so that He is not ashamed of them in the end (Luke 9:26), and to finally receive the crown of glory (1 Peter 5:4). The earth shall be full of the knowledge of the LORD!

Get Ready! Be Watchful and Pray!

You must discern the times you are in and watch for the last hour or the day of the Lord (Mark 13:37). It is important to discern the end times and to get ready. The second coming of Jesus will be sudden and unexpected as was the flood of Noah's time. You need to get saturated in the Word and spending time soaking in secret place with God to be ready.

You also need to learn to persevere and continue in the faith just as Noah did. Noah was warned and built the ark by faith, before the coming of the great flood (Hebrews 11:7). In the same way you must learn self-control and live a holy and godly life. You must continue in fellowship, showing your love to others, and encouraging one another.

Stand Still and Persevere to the End, as Your Reward is with God!

God told Daniel, "As for you, go your way till the end. You will rest, and then at the end of the days you will rise to receive your allotted inheritance." (Daniel 12:13). God prepared an everlasting inheritance to all who believe. "Praise be to the God and Father of our Lord Jesus Christ! In his great mercy he has given us new birth into a living hope through the resurrection of Jesus Christ from the dead, and into an inheritance that can never perish, spoil or fade— kept in heaven for you" (1 Peter 1:3-4). Keep your faith till the end! The end is near! **"He who is coming will come and will not delay. But my righteous one will live by faith. And if he shrinks back, I will not be pleased with him." But we are not of those who shrink back and are destroyed, but of those who believe and are saved." (Hebrews 10:37-39).**

BIBLIOGRAPHY

1. About UBS. (2008). *United Bible Societies (UBS)*. Retrieved from http://www.Biblesociety.org/index.php?id=2,

2. Compelling Facts List. *OpenDoorsUSA.org*. Retrieved from http://members.opendoorsusa.org/site/DocServer/pastorfacts_rev2.pdf?docID=2902

3. Conservative Anglicans Create Rival Church. Top leader Duncan expects to see Episcopal Church 'displaced'. (2008-12-4). *Christianity Today*, December (Web-only) 2008, Vol. 53. Retrieved from http://www.christianityto-day.com/ct/2008/decemberweb-only/149-43.0.html).

4. Earthquake Facts and Statistics. *United States Geological Survey*. (2010). Retrieved from http://earthquake.usgs.gov/earthquakes/eqarchives/year/eqstats.php

5. Easton's Bible Dictionary. Retrieved from *http://eastons-bibledictionary.com/search–salvation*

6. *eFinancialPortals*. (2010). Retrieved from http://www.efinancialportals.com/services/personal-finance-stat-sheet.aspx

7. Grady, J. Lee. (2010-11-03). Is it ok to be gay and Christian? Fire in my Bones. *Charisma.* Retrieved from http://www.charismamag.com/index.php/fire-in-my-bones/29512-is-it-ok-to-be-gay-and-christian.

8. House, H. Wayne & Price, Randall. (2003). Charts *of Bible Prophecy.* Grand Rapids, Michigan: Zondervan.

9. Hunger Stats. (2010). *World Food Program.* Retrieved from http://www.wfp.org/hunger/stats

10. Milligan, Susan. (2006-03-31). Abuse cost churches nearly $467m in '05. Settlements spiked sharply. *The Boston Globe.* Retrieved from http://www.boston.com/news/nation/washington/articles/2006/03/31/abuse_cost_churches_nearly_467m_in_05/

11. Scripture Distribution 2009. (2009). *United Bible Societies (UBS).* Retrieved from http://www.Biblesociety.org/index.php?id=21,

12. Scripture Translation. (2009). United *Bible Societies (UBS).* Retrieved from http://www.Biblesociety.org/index.php?id=22,

13. Statistics: The 21st century world. (2008, 12-04). How many unreached countries are there? Where are mission's resources going? Scripture distribution (all sources). *Howard Culbertson, Southern Nazarene University.* Retrieved from http://home.snu.edu/~HCULBERT/world.htm#abc

14. 10/40 Window: Do you need to be stirred to action? (2010-07-06). Howard *Culbertson, Southern Nazarene University.* Retrieved from http://home.snu.edu/~hculbert/1040.htm

15. Top Ten Stories of 2007. (2007-12-18). Anglican Communion fractures over Scripture, homosexuality. *Christianity Today,* January 2008, Vol. 52, No. 1. Retrieved from http://www.christianitytoday.com/ct/2008/january/2.16.html.

16. Where can I see World War 1, World War 2, and World War 3 Statistics? Three World War Statistics Compared. (2009). Three World Wars. Retrieved from http://www.threeworldwars.com/overview.htm,

17. White, Deborah. (2010-11-19). Iraq War Facts, Results & Statistics at October 30, 2010. *About.com.* Retrieved from http://usliberals.about.com/od/homelandsecurit1/a/IraqNumbers.htm

18. World Watch List. (2010, January). *OpenDoorsUSA.org.* Retrieved from http://members.opendoorsusa.org/site/DocServer/WWL2010_test.pdf?docID=5801

19. Zoll, Rachel. (2009-03-31). Catholic bishops warned in '50s of abusive priests. *Associated Press in USAToday.* Retrieved from http://www.usatoday.com/news/religion/2009-03-31-catholic-abuse_N.htm

ABOUT THE AUTHOR

Biniam Debebe is an experienced Certified Public Accountant, Certified Information System Auditor, Certified Internal Auditor, and a writer. He has earned his Masters of Business Administration (MBA) in Finance. He also studied theology at the National Bible College and Seminary for two years. He witnesses and evangelizes the Gospel of Jesus to many. He supports financially and materially orphan children and Christian ministries in different parts of the world in furthering the Gospel of Jesus. He is married to Rahel; has two children Israel and Bethel; and lives in Maryland.

FOR FURTHER
INFORMATION

For additional copies of this book
or to contact the author,
please email: lasthour2011@yahoo.com

9141706R0

Made in the USA
Charleston, SC
14 August 2011